The InterActive Classroom

Third Edition

The Complete Active Classroom Series

The InterActive Classroom, Third Edition. . .

. . . provides practical strategies for shifting the role of students from passive observers to active participants in their own learning.

The Active Teacher. . .

. . . focuses on the critically important first five days of school and becoming a proactive rather than reactive teacher.

The Active Mentor. . .

. . . gives teacher mentors practical strategies for going beyond support to actively accelerating the growth of new teachers.

The Active Classroom Field Book. . .

. . . highlights practices inspired by the bestselling *The Active Classroom*—and shows how teachers shifted responsibility for learning from themselves to their students!

The Active Workshop. . .

. . . illustrates how workshop facilitators can accelerate the continuous improvement of educators by turning attendees into active participants.

The InterActive Classroom

Practical Strategies for Involving Students
in the Learning Process

Third Edition

Ron Nash

Foreword by John Almarode

FOR INFORMATION:

Corwin
A SAGE Company
2455 Teller Road
Thousand Oaks, California 91320
(800) 233-9936
www.corwin.com

SAGE Publications Ltd.
1 Oliver's Yard
55 City Road
London EC1Y 1SP
United Kingdom

SAGE Publications India Pvt. Ltd.
B 1/I 1 Mohan Cooperative Industrial Area
Mathura Road, New Delhi 110 044
India

SAGE Publications Asia-Pacific Pte. Ltd.
18 Cross Street #10-10/11/12
China Square Central
Singapore 048423

Program Director: Jessica Allan
Content Development
    Editor: Lucas Schleicher
Senior Editorial Assistant: Mia Rodriguez
Production Editor: Andrew Olson
Copy Editor: Jared Leighton
Typesetter: C&M Digitals (P) Ltd.
Proofreader: Laura Webb
Indexer: Judy Hunt
Cover Designer: Karine Hovsepian
Marketing Manager: Deena Meyer

Printed in the United States of America.

Library of Congress Cataloging-in-Publication Data

Names: Nash, Ron.

Title: The interactive classroom : practical strategies for involving students in the learning process / Ron Nash. Other titles: The active classroom

Description: Third edition (revised edition). | Thousand Oaks, California : Corwin, [2020] | Series: The complete active classroom series | Includes bibliographical references and index.

Identifiers: LCCN 2019011891 | ISBN 9781544377711 (pbk. : alk. paper)

Subjects: LCSH: Active learning. | Learning strategies. | Project method in teaching.

Classification: LCC LB1027.23 .N37 2020 | DDC 371.39—dc23
LC record available at https://lccn.loc.gov/2019011891

This book is printed on acid-free paper.

SFI label applies to text stock

19 20 21 22 23 10 9 8 7 6 5 4 3 2 1

Contents

Visit the companion website at
http://resources.corwin.com/InteractiveClassroom
for downloadable resources.

To my classmates in the North East High School Class of 1967
forever friends
forever young
rock on

Foreword

Picture this: A teacher walks up to a student and asks him, "Where is your book?" The student, without hesitation, responds that his book is at home. The teacher responds in a frustrated tone, "Well, what is it doing there?" Without hesitation, the student quips back, "Having more fun than I am." I have no idea if this really happened, but the premise is relevant to the subsequent pages of this book. However, before reading one more word of this foreword or book, I want you to close your eyes and picture the perfect classroom. What do you see? What is the teacher doing? What are the learners doing? How would you describe the physical environment? What do you notice about the feel of the room?

My guess is that you did NOT picture students sitting in fearful silence, the teacher continuously talking, and desks arranged in symmetric rows. There may even be small pieces of tape on the floor that provide geographic markers for the arrangement of those desks. Well, Ron Nash does not picture this type of classroom, either. The classroom he pictures in his mind, and I do as well, is a classroom that is *interactive*. The teacher and the learners are interacting with ideas and concepts, facilitated by the skills and processes associated with those ideas and concepts. There is dialogue and discourse around the day's learning that moves learning forward, not just through the acquisition and consolidation of ideas but the assimilation of feedback given and received by the teacher and students. This interactive classroom is not a figment of our imaginations. The interactive classroom exists in many schools around the world.

My daughter, Tessa, is 7 years old and a very active first grader. My son, Jackson, is 4 years old and is an equally active preschool student. Having visited both of their classrooms as a parent, I have witnessed the impact of an interactive classroom on the growth and achievement of learners. This growth and achievement encompasses cognitive and social-emotional learning, not solely reserved for the benefit of standardized test scores. Yes, through their interactive classrooms they interact with reading, writing, and arithmetic but in a way that allows them to interact with their peers and teachers. They are learning to ask questions, dialogue with their peers and teachers, and make meaning of the world around them. As I said earlier, this type of learning environment is neither a figment of our imaginations nor an anomaly. However, there is still work to do.

In *The InterActive Classroom*, Ron Nash walks us through the components necessary for creating a learning environment, a perfect classroom that maximizes the growth and achievement of all learners. His extensive experience as an educator allows him to paint a picture for you that is transferrable to your own classroom by maximizing the emotional, cognitive, and behavioral engagement of all learners. This picture brings together research on how students learn with the practical application of that research to strategies and approaches to teaching and learning. From structured conversations, managed movement, music, clarity, and making thinking visible through writing, Ron Nash rips up the tape off of the floor for the rows of desks and shows us how to ensure that if your book is left at home it will NOT have more fun than the learners in the classroom.

Ron's approach is rooted in three of the most fundamental rules of engagement: (1) how you feel is real; it is the link to how you think; (2) where the mind goes, the person follows; (3) we can influence both 1 and 2. Focusing on emotional engagement,

Ron devotes significant attention to how learners feel about the learning and the learning environment (i.e., emotional engagement). How learners feel is strongly related to what they will and won't think about (i.e., cognitive engagement). After all, students won't learn from someone they don't like or in an environment they dread. So Ron describes how to get learners thinking about the right content, skills, and processes at just the right time. And what learners think about drives them to action (i.e., behavioral engagement). His approach provides clear ideas for making student thinking and learning visible through specific strategies.

This is the third edition of this book. I own the previous two editions—giving the second edition to my students at James Madison University. I would be remiss if I did not direct your attention to both the change in title and substance. First, in this third edition, the change in title from *The Active Classroom* to *The InterActive Classroom* is significant. Teachers and students can be active and not interactive. The emphasis on interactive speaks to the value Ron Nash places on the collaborative nature of learning. Second, Ron elevates the role of the teacher in this collaborative learning. By making learners' thinking visible, teachers must constantly evaluate their impact on student learning, reflect on their decisions as a teacher, and adjust when necessary to further enhance growth and achievement. These two changes will raise the bar on interactive classrooms.

Before leaving you to your own reading, reflecting, and revising of your own classroom, I want to share something personal with you. Ron Nash is my colleague, but perhaps more importantly, he is my friend. I have had the pleasure of sitting in a "classroom" and learning from Ron. He "practices what he preaches" as he creates a learning environment that embodies what he means when he says *The InterActive Classroom*. There are students across the globe who are better at reading, writing, and arithmetic because of Ron Nash. There are instructional leaders and teachers across the globe who are better in their schools and classrooms because of Ron Nash. He changed the way I set up my classroom. Although I cannot speak for them, I feel confident saying that my students are grateful. When I look at my two children, I see that they love their schools, teachers, and learning because they are blessed to be in an interactive classroom.

My hope is that you will interact with the concepts, ideas, skills, and processes in this book and experience the same success. Your learners deserve it. You deserve it too!

John Almarode, PhD
Associate Professor of Education, James Madison University
Director, Content Teaching Academy
Codirector, Center for STEM Education and Outreach

Acknowledgments

Looking back over several decades in education, it occurs to me that I must thank the teachers, administrators, and others who have shared their expertise and experience with me as a matter of course. My most rewarding years in the classroom were shared with my fellow members of the Apple Team at Plaza Middle School in Virginia Beach, Virginia, from 1992 through 1994. My colleagues in central office in Virginia Beach taught me a great deal about teaching and learning from 1994 until I retired in 2007. A special thank you goes out to Kay Burke, a wonderful author, consultant, and friend; Kay introduced me to the great team at Corwin Press, and that opened the door to a dozen years as an author and presenter.

I thank the educators who contributed to all three editions of this book with lessons and other information from their classrooms: Diana Abil-Mona, Jeff Bonine, Elise Brune, Lisa Crooks, Kathy Galford, Jennifer Henry, Melissa Martini, and Terri Myers. Thanks to Dianne Kinnison and Brian T. Jones for their wonderful illustrations.

Many thanks to Jessica Allan, Mia Rodriguez, and Lucas Schleicher at Corwin. Their ideas, guidance, expertise, and patience made it possible for me to complete this third edition of *The InterActive Classroom*.

Finally, I would like to thank my wife, Candy, for readily agreeing to my early retirement from the Virginia Beach Schools in 2007 so I could follow my dream of writing, consulting, and presenting.

About the Author

Ron Nash's professional career in education has included teaching social studies at the middle and high school levels. He also served as an instructional coordinator and organizational development specialist for the Virginia Beach City Public Schools (VBCPS) for 13 years. In that capacity, Ron trained thousands of teachers and other school division employees in such varied topics as classroom management, instructional strategies, presentation techniques, customer service, and process management. After Ron's retirement from VBCPS in 2007, he founded Ron Nash and Associates, Inc., a company dedicated to working with teachers in the area of brain-compatible learning. He is the author of 16 books for teachers and administrators. Originally from Pennsylvania, Ron and his wife, Candy, a former French teacher and administrator, have lived in Virginia Beach for the past 35 years. Ron can be reached through his website at www.ronnashandassociates.com.

Unique Features of this Book

This third edition of *The InterActive Classroom* contains features not found in the first two editions of the book. The larger trim size and lay-flat binding allows the reader to write in the margins and provide answers to questions throughout the book and, specifically, at the end of each chapter. The book should lay flat on a desk or table, allowing the reader to write easily where room has been provided.

Also, teachers get caught up in the content and grand strategy of lesson design, and tactical considerations often get overlooked. Each chapter contains tactical tips related to that content. Here is an example from Chapter 5 on "Presenting With Confidence." The tips are process related and can be used in any classroom.

Also, there is a feature called "The InterActive Classroom at a Glance" that is now available online. I have always recommended that teachers observe colleagues in classrooms throughout the building or district. Teachers tend to stay pretty insulated from what is going on elsewhere, and this means much of the great teaching and learning happening in other classrooms goes unobserved and overlooked by colleagues who could benefit from such observations. This online feature contains specific "look fors" that highlight the differences between passive classroom environments and those that are more interactive.

The emphasis throughout the book is on practicality. Teachers want things they can use tomorrow. The third edition of *The InterActive Classroom* provides engagement strategies, poses questions (rhetorical and otherwise), and presents "Tactical Tips" intended to help classrooms run smoothly.

Tactical Tip

There is a natural tendency for teachers wanting to emphasize something as particularly important to raise their voices at the end of a sentence. A student who inhabits many classrooms during the day will hear this tactic used over and over, until it becomes invisible and ineffective. Try this: When you are making an important point and want to verbally underline the last few words, try pausing for a beat, then lowering the volume of your voice. Deliver those words confidently—*and softly*. I have seen this used to great effect by professional presenters and teachers alike. It is not what students expect; *therefore, it has impact.*

Introduction

I spent my formative years in a small Pennsylvania town located on the shores of Lake Erie, in the heart of grape country. We had a movie theater on Lake Street, and my friends and I spent many a Saturday afternoon at a double-feature matinee, both movies happily sandwiched between cartoons and comedy shorts (Think Moe, Larry, et al.). In particular, we enjoyed horror thrillers like *The Werewolf*, *Bride of Frankenstein*, *Son of Frankenstein*, *Second Cousin of Dracula*, *Once Removed* (okay, okay), and other nail-biters that provided us with our fill of 1950s shock and awe.

Well in advance of the dimming of the house lights, several of us planted ourselves in the middle seats of the front row, just a few feet from the screen and therefore as close to the action as possible. With sodas and popcorn at the ready, we invited an eclectic assortment of movie monsters and villains to frighten and entertain us for hours on end. We were attendees, not participants, and that was fine with us. We did not expect to learn much, although we did come to the conclusion that a certain road-runner was unlikely to be caught by a coyote who didn't appear to be the brightest bulb in the box.

One of my favorite horror films was *The Mummy* (1959), with Christopher Lee in the title role as the rudely awakened ancient Egyptian high priest, complete with an attitude and the obligatory gauze wrapping. Lee wreaked havoc on those who disturbed his tomb and interrupted his eternal slumber, but I can assure you that my friends and I were not the least bit sleepy. Lee captivated us as he took his compliance and control world with him on his vengeful journey, naming names and settling scores. Whenever and wherever he appeared in the space of 90 minutes, he immediately had everyone's attention, including ours, on one of many long and supremely satisfying Saturday afternoons at the movies.

Same Bit Part, Different Venue

Having at last traded the front row of the cinema for the back row of a good many college classrooms beginning in 1967, I pursued my dream of teaching history. My ancient civilizations class included black-and-white educational films that were not the equal of *The Mummy* when it came to getting and holding my attention. Absent the popcorn, sodas, and gauze getup, college professors ruled our world as they took roll, then mercilessly lectured for an hour or more. One professor chain-smoked his way through a 90-minute oration twice a week, daring us to cut class or come late; skipping the lesson brought with it the penalty of lowered grades and stern looks through the smoke upon our return.

My first classroom as a teacher may well have been judged by my students a fairly ruthless place, too, minus the cigarette smoke (found only in the faculty lounge and boys' restrooms). I did get the whole stern-look thing down, come to think of it; I raised my voice and, unfortunately, lost my temper on more than a few occasions. In the manner of Christopher Lee, I strode purposefully around the set, gesticulating in a semidarkened room with a modicum of subdued lighting provided by the overhead projector. I held forth enshrouded in enough darkness and shadows to grace any horror film of the 1950s. I'm sure the reviews of my classroom in the school cafeteria at lunch included, "That Mr. Nash certainly does run to the verbose, does he not?" (or words to the like effect).

The point of this trip down memory lane is that being an attendee in the cinema—now or back in the day—is exactly what nature, the movie industry, and the makers of buttered popcorn intend. It's why each of us spent 50 cents of our hard-earned newspaper delivery income to go to Keller Theater for a weekend matinee.

In the 5 decades since my friends and I planted ourselves in harm's way a few feet from the big screen, movie audiences still seek to be entertained. The actors, directors, producers, and those behind the scenes do the heavy lifting. The rest of us just show up. Our expectation does not rise above laughing, gasping, guffawing, sobbing, or even screaming at the appropriate moments. As it was and ever has been in the world of celluloid entertainment, our task in the cinemas of the 21st century is to find a seat, settle in, settle down, deactivate our cell phones, and refrain from disturbing the other moviegoers for a couple of hours.

This semicomatose state is fine for the tiered seats of the multiplex but not for classrooms. For today's iGen'ers, being relegated to the role of attendee is simply not acceptable. They don't want to "just show up." They don't want to "settle in" for a 90-minute block, and their cell phones might actually serve to advance the cause of learning during class. And frequent academic conversations in seated or standing pairs, trios, or groups may also enhance the learning experience; no one is bothered by talking if everyone is *supposed* to talk.

> For today's iGen'ers, being relegated to the role of attendee is simply not acceptable.

Roles Not of Their Own Making

Students today do not covet—or have access to—20th-century manufacturing jobs where simply getting to work on time and doing what one is told was once *de rigueur*. The work and the workplace have changed. The world has changed. The kids have changed, and so have their expectations. The relevant word here is change.

Yet my travels over the past 2 decades have shown me time and again that too many students are still trapped in the role of attendees, for the simple reason that tradition and the status quo are hard taskmasters. Old habits die hard or, like Christopher Lee's on-screen persona, seem to live forever, even when dispatching outmoded and ineffective classroom routines to the great beyond might serve the cause of learning. In the world of education, many of these habits were brought to life in the industrial age, when control and compliance ruled the day in classrooms, in horror films, and on the factory floor.

But the industrial age has gone the way of 10-cent boxes of popcorn and nickel sodas. "The conveyer belt of the last century," write Wagner and Dintersmith (2015), "is gone. Lifetime employment with a large company is increasingly unlikely; individuals will change jobs, companies, and even professions many times in their lifetime" (p. 63). Today's students will perhaps have many jobs before they reach the ripe old age of 30; many of them will innovate their way to success and, perhaps, fortune. Witness the number of young entrepreneurs on TV and online, selling book bags, mattresses, socks, carry-on luggage, and everything imaginable.

The young are moving quickly; many of them have college credit or even college degrees before we would have graduated from high school. I listened from the back of an auditorium as a school superintendent told the story of a high school senior in his district who had created from whole cloth not one but *two* online businesses.

The good news is that districts all over the country are coming to realize that today's students will find—or create—jobs where communication and collaboration are required, along with an ability to think critically, identify *and* solve problems, write and speak with force and clarity, and work independently when necessary. Sitting in the front row, listening—or pretending to listen—to a teacher deliver information in fire hose fashion is not sufficient to prepare iGen'ers for their future in the workforce and as informed citizens in a constitutional republic. "The complexity of today's civil society places extremely high demands on citizens," assert Wagner and Dintersmith (2015, p. 68). Those essential skills (communication, collaboration, and critical thinking) will serve these future voters well.

An interactive classroom is *not* one where students sit in the front row expecting to be entertained until the movie is over or the bell rings, then hurriedly head for the exits. A dynamic and distinctly interactive classroom is filled with learning partners, including the teacher. Winston Churchill liked to say that he enjoyed learning but did not like being taught. I suspect many students today would agree with the late and long-ago British prime minister. My experience is that students who are *allowed* to be students, rather than daily guests in room 206, appreciate thinking of themselves as lead actors in their own continuous-improvement narratives. Attendees attend; participants participate—and learn. And classroom teachers learn right along with them.

> *A dynamic and distinctly interactive classroom is filled with learning partners, including the teacher.*

An Inexorable Shift

The continuum along which we as educators *at every level* should be remorselessly moving stretches from a passive, adult-centered approach where compliance and control are king to a more learner-centered classroom culture. Every teacher is, right now, *somewhere* on this continuum. Teaching doesn't take place unless learning does, and no amount of explaining, expounding, describing, pontificating, gesticulating, or entertaining on the part of a classroom teacher will result in the creation of a culture of learning.

Davis, Summers, and Miller (2012) contrast environments geared toward learning with those that have traditionally focused on "getting the work done" while keeping things under control:

> In a classroom oriented toward learning, the climate tends to have a more open, collaborative feel because students are focused on understanding. In a classroom oriented toward completing work, the climate tends to feel more burdensome with students focused on labor and production. It is important to understand that research consistently demonstrates when students approach classroom tasks with a learning orientation, their understanding of the performance of the task improves. (pp. 60–61).

Watching the body language and general deportment of students in both settings, a visitor to any classroom can immediately gauge how students feel about the situation in which they find themselves. Kids of any age know full well whether they are being cast as attendees or as participants. They know the difference between busy work and meaningful engagement in pursuit of a worthwhile goal. As they move through the grades or consider dropping out of school, thus delegating their uninvolved role to an understudy, they know when they are being shortchanged.

This, then, is where today's iGen'ers are. They don't want to mark time before "going out into the real world." They are *in* the real world. Social media and countless Internet destinations put them in the real world *right now*. Global climate disruption is pounding with increased urgency on their doors *right now*. On graduation, they will compete in tight labor markets that value 21st-century skill sets, and we as educators should help them prepare for all this right now.

Operating as participants in their own learning, students need to learn to think critically, communicate effectively orally and in writing, reflect independently and interdependently, challenge assumptions, investigate when warranted, seek feedback from multiple sources, and otherwise begin to function as serious and thoughtful citizens. No worksheet can accomplish that. No lecture is powerful enough to move the needle. No amount of classroom *efficiency* can substitute for an engaging and *effective* lesson or a project where students are fully committed to meeting a clearly understood learning goal.

> No amount of classroom efficiency can substitute for an engaging and effective lesson or a project where students are fully committed to meeting a clearly understood learning goal.

We need to meet students where they are as they—and we—look to their future and not insist they prepare for a world we once inhabited, one which no longer exists. This means educators need to move steadily and confidently along that continuum from treating students like attendees to joining them as participants and partners in the learning process. Teachers can inspire, even as they aspire to improve their own performance. The status quo needs to be revisited and overhauled. There is much about traditional education that works and works beautifully. Teachers and administrators can work together to do the hard work that comes from figuring out what to keep, what to change, what to fix, what to improve, and what to relegate to the attic with much else that we will never use.

For Whom the Filmstrip Tolls

When I began teaching in 1972, I quickly mastered all of the up-to-date technological wonders. Various projectors (overhead, filmstrip, slide) provided the visuals, while I delivered the goods on the auditory side. On behalf of the school district, I loaned each student a history textbook (out of date the minute it came off the presses and even more out of date on the back end of a multiyear book contract), and I made sure they knew where the library was (containing sets of encyclopedias even more out of date than the textbooks). With the preliminaries out of the way, I flipped the switch on the overhead projector and proceeded to give my students facts they duly recorded as notes to be consulted 30 minutes before a test or quiz.

Tradition demanded I give my eighth graders the straight skinny; in the manner of modern news organizations or blogs disseminating information to people with short attention spans, I told them exactly what they needed to know. When the school library was gutted by fire one December night, it put a serious crimp in the information flow, and it wasn't until the library was rebuilt, refurbished, and restocked that our students had access to resources beyond what we teachers doled out in 50-minute blocks of time, 5 days a week. As a history teacher, I was excited that our new library would have a recent set of encyclopedias, a new edition of the *Dictionary of American Biography*, and a brand-new atlas and globe. The library also purchased a new wooden lectern on which a dictionary the size of a riding lawnmower was perched for the use of everyone in the building. It contained all the latest words and definitions.

That was then, this is now, and this is new: We are inescapably and increasingly awash 24/7 in a sea of information, and the sources of all these data compete mightily for our attention. Information winks, blinks, and waves its arms at us in the form of advertising on our computers, and "breaking-news" bulletins crawl across the bottom of our television screens lest we miss anything. Information in the form of advertising beats us senseless before the movie starts in the local multiplex, even though we already paid to see the film. Long-lost friends resurface on social media and inform the world about what they are doing. I can listen to or watch any baseball game anywhere in the country by subscribing to a service, and I can read every statistic about every ballplayer at the click of a mouse. All the words I could ever want spelled or defined lie only a click or voice command away.

As PBL (project-based learning) gains traction nationwide, affirm Boss and Larmer (2018), adult-centered classrooms will have to give way to ever more learner-centered approaches that require more of students, *even as it changes the role of teachers*. Time must be made for projects that require students, working independently and interdependently, to do tons of research, consult with teachers and classmates, identify and solve problems, raise and then wrestle with questions, and present their findings to peers and/or adults. In a truly interactive classroom, teachers shift from being information givers to serving in a coaching role, and "their classrooms become learning environments that foster creativity, encourage student voice and choice, and promote equity by rebalancing the traditional student–teacher power relationship" (p. 162). As students move from passive observers to active participants in their own learning, they will need to develop 21st-century skills that will serve them well in the workplace and in life.

Revising the Script

So where we were not that many years ago is no longer relevant to where our students are today, and we need to acknowledge this reality, then act accordingly. As Cheryl Lemke (2010) asserts, "There is no turning back. The Internet has become integral to life in the 21st century—a place for work, play, communication, and learning" (p. 243). The students who walk into our classrooms today are quite different from those who sat at desks in my classrooms through most of my years as a teacher. Teachers and administrators can facilitate progress for students whose role shifts more swiftly than ever from passive to active. And Marc Prensky (2010) is right in saying teachers need to be partners in the learning process:

> Young people (students) need to focus on using new tools, finding information, making meaning, and creating. Adults (teachers) must focus on questioning, coaching and guiding, providing context, ensuring rigor and meaning, and ensuring quality results. (p. 10)

Teachers as learners don't need to know everything; they don't need to pretend they know everything, and they can admit this to themselves and their students. This makes teachers human, and it takes the pressure off as they shift from chief information officer to learner-in-chief in classroom

Teachers as learners don't need to know everything; they don't need to pretend they know everything, and they can admit this to themselves and their students.

environments where everyone is a partner in the learning process. Teachers and students alike can learn to actively listen in such a classroom. Teachers can model speaking *and* listening skills. In collaborative classroom settings, students can help, teach, support, and get to know and appreciate each other. Asking questions, locating information, and providing and seeking feedback can be everyone's job. Talking is thinking, and students can explain, describe, illustrate, and otherwise think out loud in classrooms where tired scripts have been revised or discarded by teachers willing to take risks on behalf of kids. And teachers can go from *broadcasting* to the room to *working* the room as accepted and valued partners in the learning process.

The Conductor's Magic

Perhaps the role of the teacher best approximates that of the orchestra conductor. The musicians make the music, but the conductor is in a position to influence the flow of the music, affecting, by her actions, the volume, tempo, and timing. She gives feedback when necessary and acknowledges effort constantly. A symphony is the ultimate collaborative effort. Everyone contributes. Everyone has different strengths and varying levels of skill; in the final analysis, the conductor figures out how to combine it all into a supremely satisfying effort. *It is at once the score, the talent, the practice, the discipline, the commitment, the passion, and the ability of the conductor to multitask and influence process that determines the quality of the performance.*

The interactive classroom is a place where the teacher effectively influences the flow of process and where his students do most of the work. It is a place where students are frequently encouraged to actively reflect on and process information, skillfully practice the art of communication, purposefully move and share, and continually engage in their own learning. Active classrooms are alternately noisy and quiet places. They are usually colorful places, and they are always safe places. *It is at once the lesson, the talent, the practice, the discipline, the commitment, the passion, and the ability of the teacher to multitask and influence process that determines the quality of the learning.*

The purpose of this book is to help teachers energize students and energize themselves in the process. My belief is that learning should be active, contemplative, dynamic, purposeful, spontaneous, safe, constructivist, brain-compatible, engaging, reflective, and *fun* for everyone involved in the process, including the person in the best position to choreograph it all—the teacher.

CHAPTER 1

The Tinkerer's Mindset

In *Built to Last* (2002), Jim Collins and Jerry Porras relate how Bill Hewlett and Dave Packard (HP) "kept tinkering, persisting, trying, and experimenting until they figured out how to build an innovative company that would express their core values and earn a sustained reputation for great products" (p. 29). Companies that are dedicated not only to great products but to exceptional customer service plant themselves in the public consciousness as entities that stand out and stand above everyone else. And they keep moving forward.

A visitor who walks through a school's front doors can draw a good many inferences concerning the state of customer service from the way he or she is greeted in the foyer and in the school office. The adults who inhabit great schools go out of their way to welcome visitors as they exhibit all the hallmarks of outstanding customer service. And even a brief walk-through with a building administrator can provide plenty of observational feedback concerning how teachers and students interact with and treat each other. A single glance through the window in a classroom door can tell an observer much about whether or not students are attendees or participants. Body language can be deafening.

For more than a decade, I coached teachers in hundreds of classrooms at all grade levels, and the most effective among them demonstrated in the classroom and in conversations with me that they loved working with—*and being with*—kids. The language they used inside and outside the classroom was the language of learning, not the language of compliance and control. The truly extraordinary teachers with whom I conferenced spoke to me of their plans, things they couldn't wait to try, a journal article that had given them a great idea or two, and risks they had taken that had paid off—or not. To a person, those teachers operated every day in the rich context of the growth mindset.

A growth mindset is not, according to Frey, Hattie, and Fisher (2018), "a state of being—it is a coping skill one chooses (or chooses not) to draw on in the face of challenge" (p. 52). Easy or familiar tasks that don't challenge us don't require this skill; we engage a growth mindset when we try something new, something different, or something potentially difficult, believing it is in the best interests of those whom we serve. Tinkering with something over and over again can expose us to failure, too, and that is a good thing. Challenges bring inevitable risks for great companies and great teachers, yet mistakes and unforced errors are necessary components of the improvement cycle.

The great teachers I have had the pleasure of observing over the course of many decades have vision; they are inspirational and aspirational role models for the students they serve, and they fully understand what they want to accomplish with and for them. Building powerful and supportive relationships with students is job one. They work to create a culture of learning, thinking, doing, experimenting, evaluating, and redoing. And they work every day to engage their students in the learning process. Learning is not a spectator sport. Learning is up close and personal. Everyone in a learner-centered classroom is a learning partner, and the chief learning partner seeks constantly to tinker, persist, and experiment in support of continuous improvement.

> *Learning is not a spectator sport.*

This is not to say that those teachers and their students don't encounter obstacles on the continuous-improvement highway. They do, and many of them have shared with me and with their students personal and professional stories of mistakes and unforced errors. But they share with a smile or a healthy dose of laughter; self-confidence and resilience are hallmarks of their success. Two important components of resilience, according to Brooks and Goldstein (2004), include the ability to set realistic goals and expectations and to learn from both success and failure. Understanding where they want to go and being perfectly capable of seeing success and failure as opportunities for growth, great teachers, like first-rate companies, never stop moving inexorably toward worthwhile goals.

Pay It Forward

Piling into a couple of school district vans many years ago, a large group of administrators and lead teachers from Virginia Beach traveled to the Craven County School District in North Carolina. We were there for 2 days, observing classrooms at every level and talking with the superintendent and his staff, all of whom took the time to have an extended lunch with us. After a lunch provided by them, they shared what they were doing in their pursuit of quality, then took our questions. When we got back home, I called the principal of the elementary school where we had spent all of the second morning. I asked if he would be willing to allow a couple of his teachers to come to Virginia Beach at our expense to present to a group of administrators. The principal came himself. He brought his assistant principal. He brought six of his finest teachers, and we had a great morning with scores of our own administrators.

Let me pause for a moment and underline this. For an entire day, *both building administrators and six excellent teachers were out of the building*, seeking to help spread the message and inspire others in a school district other than their own (and in another state). In return, the principal asked only for a small contribution to their reading program. He, his assistant principal, and six of his teachers drove more than 3 hours and stayed overnight to make that happen for us.

In January of 2019, I accompanied dozens of Corwin authors and consultants as we visited Health Sciences High and Middle College (HSHMC), an outstanding school in the poorest, most crowded section of San Diego. With a 98%-plus graduation rate, this school provides internships for students in local hospitals. Classrooms are highly interactive places filled with students who love being there. One eighth grader told me she and her friends appreciated being treated like adults and provided with assistance at every turn. Not surprisingly, a regular influx of daily visitors flocks to a school that gladly and proudly shares who they are and what they have been able to accomplish in the 12 years since its founding.

In nearly 5 decades in education, I have never failed to notice that high-performing teachers, administrators, and schools are perfectly willing to share with others the reasons for their success. They don't lock it all away, hide it under the back stairwell, or otherwise conspire to keep it a secret. They understand that continuous improvement is—and should be—a collaborative effort, not a competitive one. Education is not a zero-sum game, where I win and you must, therefore, lose. Success—along with the mistakes, unforced errors, and failures that made it possible—should be valued, celebrated, and shared with anyone willing to experiment and do some serious tinkering on behalf of children.

Education is not a zero-sum game, where I win and you must, therefore, lose.

Some Reflections on Reflecting

High-performing teachers are self-reflective. Looking at *how* they are doing *what* they are doing has become second nature. It is not a chore, nor is it something to be avoided. Improving one's performance and relevant skill sets takes time, "as well as effort, energy, and practice," write Hall and Simeral (2017). It is a "deliberate, intentional, strategic approach that signifies the importance of the key ingredient for excellence: a healthy dose of self-reflection" (p. 20). Reflection becomes the habit that keeps on giving: "*The more reflective we are, the more effective we are*," affirm Hall and Simeral (p. 21, italics in the original).

Reflecting on our practice reveals for us what is working and what needs to be adjusted, reconstructed from the bottom up, or simply discarded. When caught up in the whirlwind of multiple classroom projects and deadlines, self-imposed and otherwise, serious reflection may have to wait for calmer waters. This is where a reflective log can come in handy.

An elementary teacher once showed me her dog-eared notebook, filled with thoughts, ideas, questions, doodles, ruminations, humorous stories, and other categories too numerous to mention. I keep a reflective log on my computer when writing a manuscript or getting ready for a presentation. I'll get up in the middle of the night to write down something I will otherwise forget by morning.

> ### Tactical Tips
>
> Consider keeping a single file on the desktop of your computer, one you can easily and quickly access to add reflections on today's lessons or experiences in a reflective log. Date the entries, and revisit them when you have—or can *make*—time. Many were the occasions I thought of something I wanted to try or wanted to save for further reflection that simply disappeared because I was unwilling to take the time to capture it for later retrieval. A reflective log can be a powerful continuous-improvement tool for busy teachers and administrators.

What I Did With My Summer Vacation

Driving around town during the summer as a newly minted teacher almost 50 years ago, I would have noticed kids running, playing, socializing, laughing, and taking in a good deal of sunshine in a way that was remarkably familiar to me. Not that many years before, my friends and I would have gathered at one of several beaches on the southern shore of Lake Erie during a heat wave. A winter snowfall served as the clarion call for kids to build snow forts, play a game or two of snow football in someone's backyard, or simply pelt each other with snowballs. We were, as you may have guessed, outside more than we were inside for most of the year.

Participating in myriad neighborhood games and activities together, we worked our way through inevitable disagreements and other problems on our own, without adult supervision. And, although we did not know it then, our downtime, as Tony Wagner points out in Abeles and Rubenstein (2015), wasn't downtime at all. It was uptime. "It's in these unstructured moments that children develop essential capacities for reflective thought, creativity, social skills, and self-control." All this downtime on the part of humans, as it turns out, is "essential for healthy psychological functioning" (p. 48). For teachers, summer downtime can be uptime, with a morning or afternoon set aside for the purpose of reflecting on the just-ended school year. This investment of time can pay considerable dividends when school gets under way in August.

> *For teachers, summer downtime can be uptime, with a morning or afternoon set aside for the purpose of reflecting on the just-ended school year.*

In my early days as a teacher, I could have turned a good portion of my summer downtime into professional uptime, had I spent even a few days prior to the first week back reflecting on the ghosts of lessons past, evaluating assessments I would no doubt pull out of the drawer in due time, or exploring the best way to use primary sources in my history classroom. There are a great many things on which I could have chosen to reflect—but didn't. By not understanding the past, with a nod to George Santayana, my students and I were condemned to repeat it.

The interactive classroom can be a vibrant and productive place for teachers and students alike, but *it does not just happen*. A great deal of preparation is necessary if students are to feel safe sharing their thoughts, opinions, and ideas. Establishing procedures and routines, researching structures for communication, providing consistently high expectations, approaching discipline issues with the right mindset, providing clear instructions and directions, and building rapport and trust are all necessary to make it possible for effective and meaningful interactions to succeed.

Teachers planning for the upcoming school year (and worrying in advance about student misbehavior) can take heart in Tate's (2007) observation that any teacher's "best line of defense against behavior problems is that teacher's ability to actively engage students in meaningful and relevant lessons" (p. xiv). During the summer, questions can be raised and grappled with concerning topics like formative assessment, student collaboration, effective classroom questioning, sources of effective feedback, building relationships with students, and/or how teachers can create a culture of learning. Trying to cover the waterfront with effective teaching practices would certainly be a bridge too far, but reflecting on how to improve in one of those areas would no doubt pay dividends once the school year begins.

> *In my early years in the classroom, I never asked myself why I was doing what I was doing.*

In my early years in the classroom, I never asked myself why I was doing what I was doing. I operated in a world of *when* and *how much*. When should I show that filmstrip? How much time should I spend lecturing on the causes of the Civil War? When should I give that summative test, and how long should I make it? My contact with the other ninth-grade U.S. history teacher was limited to various social occasions and to asking him, "Where are you in the book?"

Getting Better at Getting Better

Continuous improvement is a journey, not a destination, and feedback and constant reflection are essential companions for the trip. Valuable feedback can be obtained from students and on a regular basis. California history teacher Shelly Carson, among other continuous-improvement tools, uses something called a plus/delta (+/Δ). On the plus side of a large chart, students are asked to record one thing that went really well during this past month. On the delta side of the chart, they list things that could be done to make things go better.

When Jenkins (2008) asked one of Carson's students if the plus/delta was worth doing. She replied, "Yes, because Mrs. Carson makes at least one change each month based on what we say" (p. 58). That simple, inexpensive form of feedback from her students give Carson a great deal on which to reflect. Moreover, the students *knew* she used their feedback, and that is important. If students are going to take the time to provide feedback in this manner, they want to know the teacher is really listening.

"The key to individual reflective practice," assert Hall and Simeral (2015), "is setting aside periods of time devoted to improving one's performance in the class-room. "Growth in your ability to think, reason, consider, weigh, ponder, assess, deliberate, reflect, and act on that reflection takes time, energy, and commitment" (p. 23). The best teachers I have met over several decades in education have one thing in common: They are relentless in their attempts to get better. They know they can do better; they take the time and put forth the effort to discard or fix what hasn't worked, and they are constantly trying new things, experimenting with something they heard about, read about, or that came to them in the middle of the night.

> The best teachers I have met over several decades in education have one thing in common: They are relentless in their attempts to get better.

The Synergy in Collaborative Planning

In *Academic Conversations: Classroom Talk That Fosters Critical Thinking and Content Understandings* (2011), Jeff Zwiers and Marie Crawford list and explain several advantages to face-to-face classroom dialogue between and among students. Such conversation builds critical thinking skills, promotes different perspectives and empathy, fosters creativity, cultivates connections, builds relationships, and fosters self-discovery. All these advantages apply to face-to-face collegial discussions between and among teachers and administrators. The power of reflection and conversation can be an important part of the planning process for teachers in the summer and during that first week back for staff.

I have known principals who have found the money to bring teachers together in July or even after school is out in June. Principals and central-office personnel with money to spend can invest it in conferences for teachers who demonstrate an eagerness to spend part of their summer at conferences on how the brain learns, formative assessment, analyzing data, or myriad other topics that can help teachers think about and act upon valuable information they may have less time to deal with during the school year. Administrators working with teacher leaders can hold their own conferences in the district. I took part in an online summer book club put together by the reading specialist in a rural Virginia school.

Conyers and Wilson (2016) report on a University of North Carolina study that

> suggests that collective efficacy may be functioning at its best when school districts promote and establish policies and practices that (1) support teacher collaboration, in which teachers work together to increase student achievement, and (2) nurture professional communities in which teachers feel a sense of belonging and take pride in their school, understand the school's mission, and engage in ongoing professional development to learn new strategies to support student learning. (p. 52)

Summer provides a period of time when the pressures of the school year are absent; it is the perfect time for reflection and collegial collaboration.

"When teachers combine their efforts toward a shared aim," affirm Conyers and Wilson, "they are more likely to maintain the motivation needed to persist through challenges, benefit from marshalling their individual expertise and experiences, and recognize when adjustments are necessary to accomplish their purpose" (p. 15). I became a much better teacher and learning partner when I became part of a newly formed, seventh-grade inclusion team at our middle school. When I was down, others lifted my mood. When one of us was stumped, someone else was there with a few questions or some advice. When we experienced success, we had someone with whom to share and celebrate.

This was a new, mind-opening experience for me, a teacher who had been used to going it alone for all my career up to that point, and it required a change in thinking for all of us on the team. DuFour (2015) said it best: "Educators who are accustomed to working alone, making decisions on their own, and having almost absolute power over how they manage their classrooms will need to embrace a new mindset that leads to fundamental changes in how they approach their work" (p. 181). I was introduced to a new world of collaborative planning with teachers who shared a common vision for *all* the kids on the inclusion team, and I found it an incredibly rewarding experience.

An Innovative Spirit

In my early years as a teacher, I rarely tried new things out in the classroom. Too much risk. That was unfortunate, most of all for my students. The best teachers with whom I have worked are keen to try new ideas without worrying over much that they or the ideas might not live up to expectations. James D. Hornfischer, in a book covering the last 2 years of the War in the Pacific in World War II, *The Fleet at Flood Tide* (2016), attributes to Admiral Kelly Turner this dictum: "The only thing worse than a bad idea that gets implemented is a good one that is never broached" (p. 198). We can't fail at things we don't try. For someone with a fixed mindset, avoiding failure is something to be devoutly wished. For those with a tinkerer's mindset, failure is expected, welcomed, and useful.

When teachers are excited about and fully engaged with their work and don't see it as work, their students know it, and this attitude is contagious.

A fear of taking risks or failing may hold teachers back, but there is an exciting and rewarding future out there for teachers willing to go out on the proverbial limb: "To spark the imagination and take our insights to their fullest expression," affirms Syed (2015), "we should not insulate ourselves from failure; rather, we should engage it" (pp. 210–211). When teachers are excited about and fully engaged with their work and don't see it as work, their students know it, and this attitude is contagious. When students are fully engaged with their work and don't see it as work, their teachers know it, and that is why we are all here.

Turning Talk Into Action

Here is one thing I have learned over the years: All the talent, experience, drive, enthusiasm, and synergy a building principal needs to improve systems and processes is *already in the building*. It is a matter of finding and tapping the talent and energy of staff members from the front office to the cafeteria. I also believe that those closest to the problems are closest to the solutions. New programs are often instituted at the district level but ultimately fail because the "grand plan" does not translate into action at the school level, where early involvement in the plan was nonexistent. Only a small percentage of employees buy in. The rest, including some of the most vocal, opt out. Game over.

A commitment to collaborative reflection on the part of stakeholders can surface a great deal that works well in the building—and much that doesn't. Improvement efforts are, I have found, most valued and supported when coming from the bottom up, not from the top down. When school-based or grade-level teams work collaboratively to improve performance from the classroom to the cafeteria, this represents a personal and professional commitment of those who are in the trenches and see what is needed.

At this point, it becomes a matter of what do we do about that which is broken or absent. During the necessary planning process, what steps will we take to make sure what needs to be done *actually gets done*? Talk is cheap, as the saying goes, but making things happen costs time and requires considerable effort over a long period of time. Pfeffer and Sutton (2000) suggest that organizations "have follow-up processes to ensure that decisions are implemented and that talk results in action and not just more talk" (p. 57).

In schools, building leaders (administrators and teacher leaders) will encounter criticism and other bumps in the road that can bring improvement efforts to a halt. Pfeffer and Sutton have a bit of advice for leaders facing such obstacles: "Do not accept excuses and criticisms for why things won't work or can't be done, but rather reframe the objections into problems to be overcome rather than reasons not to try" (p. 57). Obstacles are nothing if not opportunities for improvement, as any soccer or basketball coach knows. Nothing much happens unless risks are taken and mistakes made. Peters (2018) says, "Whoever tries the most stuff wins," and, "whoever screws the most stuff up wins" (p. 205).

Trying new things may well lead to messing things up, and that is true in classrooms. Interactive classrooms involve more risk than traditional, adult-centered classrooms where the information flows from the front of the room and, often, over the heads of those for whom it was intended. Reducing the amount of teacher talk, increasing the level of engagement on the part of students, giving students more responsibility, and accepting a new role as the chief partner in the learning process increases the amount of risk for teachers used to doing most of the work and, as I discovered in my very traditional classrooms, *doing most of the learning*.

The finest principals I have known were master tinkerers, willing to go out on limbs on behalf of teachers and kids. They didn't go it alone, either; they relied on teacher leaders who willingly accepted a new and sometimes difficult role as tinkerer's apprentices. The search for best practices in education need not be a lonely enterprise; my experience is that collaboration in the interest of continuous improvement brings together all the vast experience, necessary talent, unique perspectives, and useful skepticism needed to create a learning culture that benefits children and helps teachers get better at getting better in the process. And putting in place an effective continuous-improvement model built on collaboration allows new teachers and administrators to become productive learning partners going forward.

YOUR TURN

Teachers don't have to toil on, tinker, or otherwise experiment with new ideas alone. As Conyers and Wilson (2016) assert, "Teachers should accept that working together will produce gains in student learning and their own professional practice—and that every teacher can learn from and contribute to his or her fellow teachers" (p. 46). Shifting from merely congenial to collegial can make a big difference for everyone concerned, including the students. On our seventh-grade inclusion team, I can't count the times the perspectives, ideas, and experiences of various team members made all the difference in helping us achieve our goals, accentuate the positive, and accelerate student progress.

My advice to teachers and building leaders is this: Don't make improvement a solo effort, and don't wait for help to come to you. Seek others out and discover ways to make you all better teachers and to move your students forward on an improvement continuum. As customers, *that's what parents want*. If it takes a village, then call the

> *If it takes a village, then call the villagers together and let's get started, so we can meet the learning goals of students and teachers alike.*

villagers together and let's get started, so we can meet the learning goals of students and teachers alike.

Hall and Simeral (2015) list some reflective questions teachers can ponder and use on the way to disrupting the status quo of what is sometimes called silo teaching. Here are a few of them:

1. Which of your colleagues do you respect immensely?

2. Consider an area of strength in your own teaching. What other teacher shares this strength? How can you partner with this teacher to build that strength?

3. Consider an area in which you struggle. What other teacher is strong in this area? How might you partner with this teacher to bolster your skills and knowledge?

4. How can you share more frequently, openly, and deeply with your colleagues?

REFLECTIVE QUESTIONS

Can any of the previous questions be part of collaborative meetings that take place in the summer, before you and the rest of the teachers are officially required to report?

Could you meet informally over dinner or lunch in the summer at fairly regular intervals with colleagues willing to take part in some collaborative reflection throughout the course of the school year?

Building administrators are always on the lookout for emerging teacher leaders who simply don't believe in excuses and who are willing to do what it takes to move the whole school forward in the name of continuous improvement. Before the school year begins, are you willing to step up and volunteer to serve on improvement teams or lead a book club on an important topic?

Before we can move forward with any confidence, we need to know where we are right now in our practice. This is our baseline. It is neither good nor bad. It is not right or wrong. It is where we are. Are you willing to commit to a program of self-reflection and, as part of that effort, seek feedback from many sources all year long in order to get better at what you do?

As you reflect on the past school year, are there some lessons, activities, or units that are consistently successful but that would benefit from some tinkering?

CHAPTER

2

Some Assembly Required

On battlefields or soccer fields, operational plans rarely survive for long, if at all, once the action starts. And the best-laid plans of teachers can come apart quickly in the classroom. It isn't pretty when it happens, and it is often the result of a lack of preparation when it comes to procedures essential to the smooth running of activities and projects. Smith (2004) likens procedures to railroad tracks, with content as the train. If the track is laid well, the train will run smoothly (p. 82). If not, a derailment may bring things to a halt while repairs are undertaken. Classroom procedures are too important to be taken for granted; making a list and checking it twice is a start but only a start.

It is not enough to establish, advertise, and announce classroom procedures; according to Wong and Wong (2005), they must be practiced and perfected. The authors' three-step process involves first explaining the procedure, then rehearsing it, and finally reinforcing it with appropriate praise or, if it is not done correctly or quickly enough, rehearsing it again *until it becomes routine* (pp. 174–176). One reason this is so important is that students have many other teachers who have their own unique classroom procedures. If a student goes home at the end of the first day of school with six or seven sets of procedures competing for a place in his long-term memory, the second day is bound to bring confusion as he tries to remember which teachers require which procedures. The advantage goes to the teacher who quickly turns procedures into routines, ensuring that students internalize procedural habits that will serve them well all year long.

Lisa Crooks, a first-grade teacher at Great Bridge Primary School (Virginia), devotes a good deal of time during the first 19 days of school to "routines, routines, routines." Crooks approaches math in a rotation approach that has students working independently or interdependently and which includes hands-on activities and a technology component. Leaving a station clean and ready for the next group is not possible without a quick and efficient clean-up procedure. A useful trigger for this is music. Crooks does not have to spend time telling groups of students to move to the carpet for a whole-class meeting; the music does that for her (personal e-mail, 1/24/19).

A classroom devoted to hands-on learning and collaboration requires gobs of dedicated space for meetings, movement, pairing, and sharing. As can be seen in Figure 2.1, Lisa Crooks has no teacher's desk or dedicated teacher space. Every bit of space is devoted to student engagement. And, as I observed one January morning, Crooks supports that engagement with effective and efficient classroom routines.

When Plans Go Plop

Unless the routines are well established in a classroom, students will find it difficult to make the right choice every time. It is understandable that, left to their own devices or in the absence of clear, practiced procedures, students can—and will—get into trouble. Juxtaposition students who are in a passive mode for too long with the absence of established and practiced procedures, and even the most innocent act can lead to difficulty.

Figure 2.1   Lisa Crooks's First-Grade Classroom. Note the large spaces and walkways for movement.

Source: Photo by Kathy Galford.

As an example, let us consider the pencil sharpener, a wonderful invention, to be sure, and still necessary today despite a spate of laptops. This seemingly innocuous and indispensable contrivance can be a flashpoint for a very good reason. Let me illustrate with a story that may strike a chord with middle or high school teachers:

Picture young Eddie sitting quietly in his seat near the classroom windows. His notebook is open, his pencil is in his hand, but his mind wanders. He has been sitting listening to a lecture on something or other for perhaps 20 minutes. Eddie is restless and bored. Moreover, he knows there is a full half-hour left in the class period . . . and then his eyes make contact with the pencil sharpener, a legitimate destination for a student if ever there was one. Eddie's cortex begins to function again as he works out the approximate distance and the available routes. He is not aware of any official policy for sharpening the pencil in this classroom, but a trip to the pencil sharpener certainly seems justified, since his pencil is dull and taking notes is, he reasons, important. Others, on occasion, have made the trip without comment from the teacher, although he can remember the teacher stopping once and staring pointedly at Marty all the way to the sharpener. Might get the stare, then, but a definite plus for the trip is that the route he has mapped out will take him past Betsy. It also takes him past his archenemy, Tony, but passing Betsy in the process makes it worth throwing the dice. He gets up, heads for the sharpener, gets tripped by Tony, falls over Betsy's desk . . . well, you get the idea.

Suffice it to say, then, that the consequences for not establishing, explaining, rehearsing, and reinforcing basic procedures can interfere with or effectively prevent the smooth functioning of the classroom. The active classroom has at least *one powerful advantage* for anyone who has Eddie and a pencil sharpener in the same room. Eddie's original reason for going to the pencil sharpener had nothing whatever to do with his pencil, his notes, or the lecture. He had been sitting for 20 minutes, and he needed to move. His brain's cortex went to work not on the lecture content but on *how he could get up and GO somewhere.* The pencil sharpener just happened to come into his line of sight.

> *The consequences for not establishing, explaining, rehearsing, and reinforcing basic procedures can interfere with or effectively prevent the smooth functioning of the classroom.*

In a fully functioning interactive classroom, Eddie would not have found himself sitting still for 20 minutes. He would have been engaged in a standing pair share with someone (maybe even Betsy) a good deal sooner. A gallery walk might have sent the fidgets packing for Eddie. The whole trip to the pencil sharpener and its consequences amounted to a symptom of two larger problems: (1) the lack of established, practiced, and completely familiar procedures and routines and (2) an overabundance of seat time.

Reflecting on the best way to handle basic procedures can be done during the summer months. Ideas can also be shared with colleagues who have a reputation as someone whose classroom is both efficient and effective. There are questions that need answering that we think can wait until that first week back for teachers, but my experience is that those busy days and nights are filled with paperwork and myriad things planned for teachers by the powers that be. Any teacher who, again, working alone or with someone else, takes the time to record and ponder procedures and processes that will either facilitate—or serve as a roadblock to—the smooth running of the classroom, is ahead of the game. The answer to questions as simple as *What is the procedure for sharpening a pencil?* or *What visual or verbal cue will I use to get my students' attention?* will go a long way toward keeping the train on the track all year long. Deal with it now, or deal with it later.

List below some procedures that may require explaining, practicing, evaluating, and adjusting:	4.
	5.
1.	6.
2.	7.
3.	8.

The Work in Working Relationships

Many teachers love children and care for them deeply, yet in some cases, their classrooms are dysfunctional places where chaos impedes instruction and continuous improvement. Students must learn to respect and value classmates, and teachers cannot assume students come to class with a working set of collaborative skills (including those related to active and empathetic listening). If students are openly disrespectful of one another, working the room on a daily basis for the teacher becomes a matter of putting out constant fires and dealing with conflict as students who should be collaborating with classmates are doing anything but. If working collaboratively is essential for today's students—and tomorrow's workers and citizens—teachers need to commit to effective, productive, and positive classroom environments. Effective collaboration requires equally effective *working relationships* between and among students and teachers.

> *Effective collaboration requires equally effective working relationships between and among students and teachers.*

These relationships are necessary if students are going to meet and work in pairs or groups on a regular basis—face to face or online. This begins with the building of effective teacher–student relationships. "When students experience healthy, growth-producing relationships with their teachers," assert Frey, Fisher, and Smith (2019), "they are more likely to mirror those actions and behaviors with their peers." The authors point out that modeling is not enough: "By teaching students to engage with peers and develop respect for one another, we provide them with avenues for dealing more productively with problems" (p. 97). Absent these important relationships, interactions between and among students and their teachers are likely to founder and, ultimately, fail completely.

Teachers need to understand the difference between cooperation and collaboration and communicate this to students. I did a short stint in a machine shop between my junior and senior years of college, and for most of that summer, I ran a drill press and a punch press. The employee to my left gave me several pieces of metal, and I drilled or punched holes in them, then handed them off to someone else. We *cooperated*, of course, or the chain would have been broken and the product would have gone unfinished. We did *not*, however, collaborate in any real sense. We, as workers, were as interchangeable as the machines we used to construct the *product du jour*. We simply followed orders; if one of us was absent, someone else filled in . . . and the show went on. Cooperating is far simpler, frankly, than collaborating successfully.

The educational system of the last century did a good job of preparing workers for industrial-age jobs like the one I held during those three months in 1971. Indeed, as Trilling and Fadel (2009) point out, "Standardization, uniformity, and mass production were important to both the factory and the classroom" (p. 13). The passive climate of secondary schools in the 20th century may have helped students learn to cooperate, but it certainly did nothing to build the kind of often-complicated working relationships that are necessary for good joint efforts when it comes to complex tasks and projects in highly interactive classrooms. Today's employers are looking for that collaborative mindset. Robinson (2011) maintains that 21st-century companies "want people who can think creatively, who can innovate, who can communicate well, work in teams and are adaptable and self-confident" (p. 69). The implications for modern classrooms should be clear; students need to learn to work closely and effectively with peers—and with teachers.

Collaboration "involves people working together in a shared process in which their interaction affects the nature of the work and its outcomes" (Robinson, 2011, p. 235). The degree to which members of a team can—or cannot—work together may play a large role in whether the problem is solved, the product is finished, or the company is ultimately successful. The mission statement of the D-School (design school) at Stanford University, as cited in Brunner and Emery (2009), begins with this sentence: "*We believe true innovation happens when strong multidisciplinary groups come together, build a collaborative culture, and explore the intersection of their different points of view."* Often, however, what gets in the way of success is a set of partners who *"cannot get along well enough or long enough to see the fruits of the collaboration"* (Brunner & Emery, 2009, pp. 97–98, italics in the original). A look at the business landscape today is enough to convince even a casual observer that a failure to collaborate has been the death of many a company or organization. In schools, many teachers will create groups and then turn them loose with a set of instructions and an admonition to respect one another as they work together toward the completion of an assignment.

The skills needed by students tasked with working in a collaborative fashion "don't magically appear when the students need them" (Johnson, Johnson, & Holubec, 1990, p. 89). The skills involved in active listening must be learned, and teachers *must facilitate* that learning. "Cooperative skills need to be taught directly and practiced repeatedly," writes Costa (2012). "Listening, consensus seeking, giving up an idea to work on someone else's idea, empathy, compassion, leadership, knowing how to support group efforts, altruism—all are behaviors indicative of intelligent human beings" (p. 247). But Costa points out that the competitive nature of many students, narrow points of view, egocentrism and ethnocentrism, and a tendency on the part of many to criticize the values, emotions, and beliefs of others all must be dealt with by teachers who want students to work together in a spirit of cooperation.

> *The skills involved in active listening must be learned, and teachers must facilitate that learning.*

If there is a key ingredient in the effective operation of interactive classrooms, it is listening. Listening skills (including paraphrasing, asking questions to provide clarification, using supportive body language, pausing to allow the speaker and the listener time to think, and summarizing, to mention a few) are not often taught. Students who don't understand what active listening entails can be excused if they go to a better place in their minds while teachers or partners talk—pretending to listen replaces active listening. "Unfortunately," write Frey, Fisher, and Smith (2019), "for a lot of students, the opposite of speaking is waiting to speak again, rather than listening" (p. 102). These important skills need to be explained, modeled, and practiced in classrooms. Active listening is a critical communication skill, but it is often overlooked or taken for granted. If teachers want students to work in effective collaborative groups, then listening skills must be frontloaded. Again, some assembly is required.

Here are some questions students can answer and discuss with classmates in seated or standing pair shares. Their conversations can be followed by some whole-class sharing.

- Why are good working relationships between and among teachers and students important in the classroom?

- How can students support each other when working in pairs or groups?

- What does it mean to respect others?

- How can we best support a classmate who has just made an obvious mistake in public?

Embrace the Motivators

Rogers and Renard (1999) affirm that "students are motivated when they believe that teachers treat them like people and care about them personally and educationally.

[Teachers need to] foster relationships that help students see teachers as teachers and not as dictators, judges, juries, or enemies" (p. 34). Having worked with more than 50,000 students in the United States, the Netherlands, and Australia over a 15-year period, Wubbels, Levy, and Brekelmans (1997) came to the conclusion that "relationship-building is a prerequisite to a positive classroom climate. Without this piece of the repertoire, teachers cannot fully develop in their practice" (p. 85). Teachers need to consistently work at developing relationships with students and their parents from the very beginning of the school year. As a teacher coach, I have seen the benefits of this at all grade levels and in all subject areas; teachers who invest in powerful working relationships will find the going easier and more rewarding.

As a new middle school teacher, I set a goal of talking with all my students' parents during the teachers' week in August, and no one will be surprised to discover these calls spilled over into the first week or two of school (having bitten off a more than I could chew in the available time). As students began to talk with their classmates at lunch during those first couple of days, it became common knowledge I was randomly calling parents every evening. I had several students ask me when I was going to call *their* parents. They knew these calls were positive, and I worked hard each evening trying to contact as many parents and guardians as possible. The payoff came later in the year when I had to make a different kind of call; these parents knew me by then, and the 10- or 15-minute conversation we had back in August or early September paved the way for a much smoother conversation in November.

I had also taken a few notes on index cards during those first calls, and the information I garnered concerning student weaknesses and strengths, as well as what they loved doing in their spare time, helped immeasurably during the school year. Based on one long conversation with the mother of a dyslexic student, the special education teacher and I were able to help her son with his writing right out of the gate in September. The fact that we were willing to invest so much in his progress made *him* eager to do well, and his writing improved a great deal over the course of the year, and his mother appreciated the effort and the results. Everyone on our team understood the importance of building solid working relationships early on, and those relationships helped facilitate the continuous improvement process for our students. That year was my most satisfying as a teacher, and there is no doubt in my mind that our decision as a team to invest in those working relationships with parents contributed enormously to our success.

Students who observe negative behavior on the part of the teacher can conclude that negative behavior is perfectly acceptable in that teacher's classroom.

Teachers who demonstrate by their actions that relationship building is important to them and to the effective operation of the classroom environment have a much better chance of making it all work. Students who observe negative behavior on the part of the teacher can conclude that negative behavior is *perfectly acceptable* in that teacher's classroom. A teacher who loses her temper consistently should expect students in her classroom to lose theirs. Jones (2007) provides teachers with a maxim that is essential for success in any classroom: "Calm is strength, Upset is weakness" (p. 180).

The teacher who gets upset will downshift from the cortex to the brainstem (Burke, 2008). In the brainstem, problem solving and decision making are no longer possible, although the teacher desperately needs to be able to think clearly and act responsibly. According to Jones, "When you are calm, you can bring all of your wisdom, experience, and social skill to bear in solving a problem. When you become *upset* and downshift, none of that knowledge or wisdom is available to you. As the saying goes, 'My life is in the hands of any fool who can make me angry'" (p. 180).

Student interaction can lead to disagreements between partners in a discussion or other collaborative activities. Risking this kind of frequent interaction means that the teacher must model remaining calm and should avoid getting upset in the face of conflict. It may mean pausing and breathing deliberately a couple of times before proceeding. The breathing causes the teacher to relax, and according to Bailey (2001), "Conscious, slow deep breathing brings more oxygen to our lungs and our brains for greater clarity, calmness and energy" (p. 40). I have observed teachers who remain calm and refuse to be manipulated by students; more often than not, those classrooms function smoothly and efficiently on a daily basis.

In building powerful working relationships, one tool that is often misused, yet should not be overlooked, is praise. Todd Whitaker (2004) credits Ben Bissell (1992) with a description of five things that make praise more effective. Praise must be, according to Bissell (1992), authentic, specific, immediate, clean, and private (pp. 46–47). The last descriptor is particularly important in the classroom. Some students do not like public praise, and praising someone who likes their accolades delivered in private may be a demotivator. There is a business maxim called the Platinum Rule, which says that we should do to others as they would have done to themselves. This is true of praise. Publicly praising a student who prefers private recognition may cause him or her to shut down for a long time, maybe for the rest of the year.

Teachers will often give praise in phrases like "Good job!" or "Excellent work!" Praise that is this general is less effective than that which is specific. According to Costa (2008), "What makes an act 'good' or 'excellent' must be communicated along with the praise. Thereby, the student understands the reason or criteria that make the act acceptable and thus the performance can be repeated" (p. 214). (See Figure 2.2.)

A teacher, then, must be consistently positive and work *ceaselessly* to build positive relationships. As we have seen, this may begin in late summer with parents and should continue throughout the course of the school year with students and parents alike. In addition, the teacher must show that remaining calm in the face of conflict or frustrating situations is the best way to deal with both. Genuine and unceasing efforts to build rapport will help build trust, an essential ingredient in the interactive classroom.

Avoid the Demotivators

In *What to Do With the Kid Who . . .* , Kay Burke (2008), in a chapter dealing with classroom climate, lists 12 teacher behaviors that can quickly and effectively dismantle trust as it erodes the climate of the classroom. Doing these things would be bad enough in a classroom where students are passive observers, but the effect of many of these in an interactive classroom would be like shouting in an echo chamber. The teacher who asks students to share frequently in pairs or groups is asking for trouble if she models inappropriate behavior herself.

In Figure 2.3, I have listed Burke's (2008) "Dirty Dozen" in the left column, and I have indicated in the right column what *I believe* would be the effect of these behaviors on a class where students are expected to talk, move, and collaborate frequently (p. 87).

Figure 2.2 Examples of Praise: Inappropriate and Appropriate

Example 1—Inappropriate Praise	Example 1—Appropriate Praise
The teacher passes by Tony's desk while students are working and slaps Tony on the back, saying, "Great work on your essay, Tony!"	The teacher crouches next to Tony while students are working and says quietly, "Tony, I just gave you some feedback on the essay you turned in this morning and I noticed that your verb-subject agreement was correct in every paragraph. That is a definite improvement from last week's essay. I thought you might want to know."
In the situation above, the praise is general, and no helpful feedback is given to Tony. The reason for the praise may remain a mystery forever, or at least until the essay is returned.	In the example above, the teacher gives Tony some specific feedback from the essay. The feedback may be cause for a bit of celebration on Tony's part, and it may ensure that Tony looks for verb-subject agreement in the future.
Example 2—Inappropriate Praise	**Example 2—Appropriate Praise**
The teacher stops class and has every-one applaud Tina because her grade over the last two similar assignments improved one full letter grade. Tina turns red and covers her face with her hands.	While students are working quietly on an in-class assignment, the teacher motions for Tina to come up front, where, very quietly, he informs her of the good news . . . that her grades are steadily improving. He also gives several concrete reasons for her improvement over time.
This is inappropriate if Tina is the kind of person who hates public praise. Before giving praise publicly, a teacher should know that the object of the praise is okay with it.	The praise here is not only private, but specific. It also gives Tina a chance to ask some questions, but quietly and with no chance of anyone overhearing the discussion.

These demotivators can cause stress levels to rise significantly. Teachers who regularly scold students and use sarcasm, or whose behavior in the classroom is consistently negative, put students in a position where they find it difficult to learn. Sylwester (1995) affirms that "high cortisol levels can lead to the despair we feel when we've failed" (p. 38). Further, *chronically* high cortisol levels "can lead to the destruction of neurons associated with learning and memory" (Sylwester, 1995, p. 38). As Bluestein (2001) points out, students who are continually anxious and stressed out can be at considerable risk and may choose to disengage altogether and finally drop out of school: "Clearly, a stressful school environment interferes with its instructional objectives" (p. 33).

Teachers who are consistently positive and have rid their classrooms of sarcasm, negativity, scolding, threats, and other demotivators will be much more successful in establishing and maintaining a climate conducive to learning.

Frequent encouragement on the part of the teacher is paramount. Students must know you believe that they can and will succeed. In an interactive classroom, everyone is involved, not just a small and predictable group of regular players. "When you fail to recognize particular students, you can communicate a low level of confidence in their abilities" (Boynton & Boynton, 2005, p. 8). This may mean that teachers have to limit the number of times they call on individuals in class. Grinder (2000) affirms that it is perfectly acceptable *to the rest of the class* for one individual to ask a couple of questions, but "after the same student has asked several questions, the teacher has the class' permission to delay answering the questions" (p. 35). One way of dealing with this situation

Figure 2.3 Adaptation of Kay Burke's Dirty Dozen "Demotivators"

Behavior	Effect in the Active Classroom
Sarcasm	Students will not only be hurt by such sarcasm on the part of the teacher, but will use it themselves when they meet in pairs or groups. Sarcasm or humiliation from any source will inhibit the kind of student interaction necessary in the active classroom.
Negative tone of voice	This will not only turn students off, but it will encourage their own use of such negativity in their own discussions.
Negative body language	Any teacher who is working with students on presentation skills will, at some point, have a discussion on body language. Telling students to be careful of negative body language and then modeling precisely that reveals inconsistencies that will undermine the effectiveness of any discussions or group collaboration.
Inconsistency	Teaching one thing and modeling something else is an example of an inconsistency that can lead to trouble. Procedures need to be consistent as well.
Favoritism	In a classroom where the teacher may ask students to scribe or perform other procedural duties, calling on the same person all the time will backfire.
Put downs	Insulting students (intentionally or not) will erode trust and, once again, set the stage for students to do the same thing when they are in pairs or groups.
Outbursts	Even short bursts of temper model inappropriate behavior, and such outbursts serve to make the other students in the room feel unsafe. If the behavior is repeated, the fact that they could be the next recipient of an outburst or tirade may never be far from their minds.
Public reprimands	If needed, reprimands should be administered in private. The interactive classroom requires students to talk and share frequently. Being humiliated by the teacher will lead to embarrassment that will carry over into the collaborative activities the teacher is working so hard to put in place. It may also be mimicked by students in the class.
Unfairness	As Burke suggests, "Taking away promised privileges; scheduling a surprise test; 'nitpicking' while grading homework or tests; or assigning punitive homework could be construed as 'unfair,'" and the negativism among students is sure to carry over into any of the interactive activities the teacher has planned, with unintended, but predictable, results (p. 91).
Apathy	The teacher in an interactive classroom is in the role of orchestra conductor. Imagine a conductor whose whole demeanor during practice and a performance is apathetic. If the conductor doesn't seem to care, why should the members of the orchestra . . . or the apathetic teacher's students?
Inflexibility	Teachers must be willing to make adjustments in the classroom based on the needs of the students or on changing circumstances that would affect performance if the change or adjustment is not made.
Lack of humor	Humor is a key ingredient to success in the active classroom. Teachers, as Burke points out, need to be able to laugh at themselves. Being able to do that encourages students who are sharing frequently to do the same. Burke is right on the money when she says that "humorless classes lack energy" (p. 91). I have found that humorless teachers lack energy as well. Teachers do not have to be naturally funny to use humor. Appropriate jokes, funny stories, and self-deprecating humor are all valuable tools.

Source: Adapted from Burke (2008, p. 91).

is to let the student who keeps asking questions—and by so doing, dominates the proceedings—know that there will come a time his or her latest question will be answered, perhaps one on one once the class is engaged in something else or after class.

Shifting from passive to active mode, then, involves not inconsiderable risks on the part of students. Before they are willing to participate in the sharing and interpersonal

> *Before they are willing to participate in the sharing and interpersonal communication that is the lifeblood of the interactive classroom, kids need to know it is safe for them to do so.*

communication that is the lifeblood of the interactive classroom, kids need to know it is safe for them to do so. It is the job of the teacher to provide that safe environment. Teachers need to be aware of undercurrents of tension or conflict that can distress or hurt children. In the words of Bluestein (2001), "Kids need to know that an adult will be there for them, and that we are capable of intervening and supporting them without making things worse. This means learning to listen, pay attention, and take kids seriously in ways that perhaps we never have before" (p. 286).

Creating a plan to help students with very basic social skills may be necessary before students can share with each other effectively and productively. Bosch (2006) suggests that teachers "have students role-play, read books for discussion on social issues and behaviors, or establish a list of positive ways to communicate with one another" (p. 64). Establishing a set of behavioral expectations for pair, group, or class interaction during the first week of school will pay great dividends later in the year, but only if the teacher sees to it that everyone (including him or herself) lives up to those expectations.

YOUR TURN

As you plan for the coming school year, there are some questions related to procedures and routines, along with the building of working relationships between you and your students (and between and among your students), the answers to which will go a long way toward the smooth functioning of your classroom.

Here is an example: **How will you get the attention of students when they are talking or collaborating on an activity?** This seems simple enough, but I have watched as teachers try one method after another to bring students back, only to fail every time. I once observed as the teacher finally gave up and stood with her arms crossed in silence by a radiator. The students stopped talking immediately—*because she wasn't.* Silence, as it so

often does, served that teacher well, and it was completely unintended. As an observer, I often come to the conclusion that the teacher is winging it, casting out one cue after another with no results. When there is no one tried-and-true method of getting their undivided attention, teachers are left to improvise, and that is not efficient.

I have made that question the first of many over the next two pages, leaving room for teachers to reflect on those things that will help things run smoothly and efficiently in a culture replete with student-to-student conversations, collaborative activities and projects, frequent peer feedback, and the kind of self-regulation on the part of students that increases cooperation, even as it decreases tension and uncertainty.

REFLECTIVE QUESTIONS

What one way will you use—and practice until everyone has it down—to get the attention of your students, no matter what they are doing? (Coach Vincent Lombardi believed that practice doesn't make perfect. Perfect practice makes perfect. Keep using this one way of bringing students back until it doesn't work; then, practice it some more until it does.)

What can you do to memorize names quickly, then get to know what makes students tick? (I know elementary teachers who learn the names of their students in one day. "Greeting people by their names," write Bradberry and Greaves (2009), "not only acknowledges them as the essence of who they are, but also allows you to become connected to them in more than just a superficial way"

(p. 140). Teachers who memorize and use names early on have an advantage over those who don't take the time or make the effort to do so.)

What kinds of positive body language will help you establish and build rapport with students? (I once observed a teacher who paced back and forth with crossed arms and what seemed like a permanent frown, something that was not conducive to building any kind of rapport. Indeed, his body language said he would rather be somewhere else. His students' body language said the same thing. Game over.)

When students need materials at some point, how will that be accomplished on a regular basis? (One middle school teacher uses a piece of upbeat music to get her students to and from where the materials were kept. This gave them a chance to move, sending more oxygen and glucose to the brain.)

If returning the room to the way it was when students entered is a priority, how will you accomplish that on a regular basis? (I have known teachers who played a certain song that put kids in motion bringing order to the classroom before leaving or after an activity or lab. They played that song only for that purpose.)

In the event you have a substitute teacher take over for you at some point, what can you do to make sure things run smoothly? (A seventh-grade U.S. history teacher called me the night before her absence, and we discussed how I could best cover the material as her substitute without resorting to worksheets. I suggested something I thought might work. She agreed, and it worked out well. Seeking a substitute who has some knowledge of the content area, then communicating with that person concerning expectations and possibilities, can benefit students and the sub.)

Incorporating Structured Conversations

If talking were actually teaching, it follows that the more we talk the more students learn, but this simply isn't the way it works. Were it so, my students would have passed every test while demonstrating an in-depth knowledge of the history of our nation—something I can assure you was not the case. By doing most of the talking in my classes, I displaced timewise any opportunities my students might have had to develop their own communication and critical-thinking skills as they processed content.

Prensky (2010) conducted more than a thousand interviews with students from around the world and confirmed they don't want to be lectured to; they *do* "want to work with their peers on group work and projects . . . ." The students he interviewed also "want to create, using the tools of their time" (pp. 2, 3). Too often today, the tools remain in the hands of teachers, and students are once again relegated to the role of passive observers while a teacher with a brand-new electronic whiteboard seems to be having all the fun. "When students are communicating and collaborating (and talking)," says Juliani (2018), "much more learning is happening!" (p. 29). Breaking out of passive-classroom mode and moving toward a more project- and student-centered approach requires that teachers spend a good deal of time planning how they can harness the power of collaboration, communication, critical thinking, and creativity.

Skills involving speaking and listening are highly prized today. In the global economy, employers need employees who can effectively communicate (Bracey, 2006). In the 21st century, workforce skills include being "able to work comfortably with people from other cultures, solve problems creatively, write and speak well, think in a multidisciplinary way, and evaluate information critically" (Gewertz, 2007, p. 25). Kagan (1994) reminds us that "students of today must learn to communicate and work well with others within the full range of social situations, especially within situations involving fluid social structures, human diversity, and interdependence" (p. 2:6).

Teachers and school districts must begin to recognize that so-called "soft skills" are critical when it comes to our students' futures. Future employees who may be expected to collaborate successfully while creating new products, identifying and solving problems, making decisions, and dealing with customers (and each other) must practice communicating and collaborating in school. Teachers must shift the communications workload from themselves to their students. Talking is not teaching; talking is thinking, and thinking is learning.

> Teachers and school districts must begin to recognize that so-called "soft skills" are critical when it comes to our students' futures.

Making Time to Process New Information

I do enjoy listening to a good speaker, and educators who find the time (and the money) to attend educational conferences have the opportunity to hear and see many wonderful keynote sessions. These speakers are in great demand—and for good reason. They have spent a good deal of time becoming experts in this or that education-related subject, and they have a lot to say. We listen to the speaker, jot down whatever notes we can, buy the book, and leave the conference having been inspired and challenged.

The one thing we often can't do, however, is process the information in small chunks as it is being delivered. Because of the time restrictions placed on the presentation, at best we can commit to reading the book and looking at the handout or notes at some point down the road, on our own time as we individually reflect on the topic. The shelves in many office bookcases sag under the weight of binders, books, handouts, and notes from long-ago conferences.

If we're lucky after a keynote speech, we may bump into someone who was in attendance and, over coffee, is willing to share a few notes and impressions from the session. I find these informal, postkeynote encounters extremely helpful because the person with whom I am reflecting may have a different perspective than I do, and sharing our own views and perspectives may lead me to a slightly different understanding of what we both saw and heard that day. He or she may have taken more notes than I or caught something I did not catch during the speech. Even a relatively short period of collaborative reflection is useful and enlightening.

> *Even a relatively short period of collaborative reflection is useful and enlightening.*

These keynote addresses are sometimes followed by question-and-answer sessions in which educators can begin to process the information, clear up any misunderstandings, ask for points of clarification, and begin to process the information with other educators during that time. During these follow-up sessions, as well as over coffee-fueled conversations, we really ramp up our thinking as we talk with others and share perspectives, information, and ideas. Allen and Hann (2011) make the point that "most of us get our best insights, understanding and ideas about new information from talking about it with other people" (p. 36). In the course of a day, then, conference attendees can benefit from the perspectives of other educators as they compare notes and share their own experiences in ways that enrich the conversations and deepen understanding. For those not lucky enough to connect with others, what was said during the sessions may simply fade and then disappear.

Oral language skills are often neglected in favor of reading and writing for the simple reason that speaking and listening are not tested, while reading and writing clearly are. But Zacarian (2013) maintains that if we want students to be literate, we should not limit our coverage and our efforts to reading and writing alone:

> Literacy is connected to four domains: listening, speaking, reading, and writing. As teachers, we often think of reading and writing as the academic side of literacy. However, listening and speaking are truly essential connection makers. They connect speaking to writing and listening to reading. For this to occur, we have to consider how to make this an active process. (p. 103)

Tactical Tip

If you are seated at a large, round table or in more classroom-style seating provided by the hotel at a conference or workshop, identify one or two participants and chat with them a bit before things get underway. When the session is finished, invite them to have a cup of coffee somewhere close, and compare notes. Talk about what you heard, and get their perspectives. This conversation, even if it lasts only until the coffee is gone, will help you remember—and perhaps better understand—what you all just heard and saw. If you simply go to another session before processing this one, you are much less likely to remember much. An unintended consequence of one such impromptu conversation years ago was that I was able to learn more about what my new acquaintances were doing in their district, and I shared what we were trying to accomplish. I took more notes from that discussion than I had done in the keynote.

These student-to-student paired or group conversations are useful laboratories for thinking and processing new information, and it follows that students who benefit from these discussions (and the perspectives of others) will find writing about the topic or concept easier.

When I suggest students need more practice in having conversations with peers, teachers often roll their eyes; clearly those teachers have had more than their share of lunch duty. But simply talking with friends informally and learning to speak and listen with some facility are two different things. Listening is often the key to understanding, yet educators have little or no training in how to actively listen. Listening, says Zwiers (2008), "requires thinking, not just hearing" (p. 118). For students talking in pairs or groups, active listening involves asking questions and summarizing. It means taking turns and being at all times respectful and empathetic. Listening includes supportive body language and periods of silence so everyone can arrange his or her thoughts. Communicating effectively at any level or in any content area is not easy, and for students to become proficient in these areas, they need practice.

> *For students talking in pairs or groups, active listening involves asking questions and summarizing.*

Life in the "Telling" Classroom

Discussing something with a partner or in a small group can be a stimulating experience, yet in many classrooms, students are expected to sit quietly while a teacher fills the role of the keynote speaker, with a one-way flow of information and precious little time, if any, for either independent or interdependent processing. There is no formal question-and-answer period built in to this process; the bell rings and students fill the hallways headed for another class, another subject, and another speaker/teacher. This kind of educational model is, asserts Lent (2012), "not only obsolete but damaging. Students in such classes report a lack of interest in subject matter and decreased motivation to learn more than is required for a passing grade" (p. 19). For students who couldn't care less about the passing grade, life in what Prensky (2010) calls the "telling classroom" is likely to be less than stimulating or inspirational.

Once again, I go back to our experiences as adults in professional development sessions that can last an entire morning or afternoon—or even a full day. I often ask teachers who have attended such sessions if they have ever gone to a better place in their minds 10 minutes or so into the proceedings. Without fail, almost every hand goes up, and everyone laughs. Many of their faces betray a certain sense of guilt because we aren't really *supposed* to go to a better place in our minds after 10 minutes, are we? Not really, but we do! The brain, according to Jensen (2005a), "is poor at nonstop attention. It needs time for processing and rest after learning" (p. 37). Jensen recommends that periods of direct instruction be held to 5 to 8 minutes in the primary grades and 12 to 15 minutes at the secondary level.

In too many classrooms, this extended one-way flow of information is still in play. The authors of one study, cited in McTighe and Seif (2010), looked at about a thousand fifth-grade students in 737 science classrooms across the United States. They found that those fifth graders spent "91 percent of their time listening to the teacher or working alone, usually on low-level worksheets" (pp. 154–155). In a world where problem solving and critical thinking are more highly valued than ever and in a democracy where those skills are equally important, we simply cannot afford the kind of passive classrooms we have inherited—and carried over—from the last century.

As social studies coordinator for a large district many years ago, I facilitated the purchase of middle school history textbooks, at great expense to the school district. Teachers who are handed the teacher's edition of an expensive textbook may rightly assume it is intended to be the centerpiece of a curriculum that may seem just as daunting and expansive. Lent (2012) correctly points out that teachers "come close to having a panic attack when they count the days left in the year and the topics left to 'cover'" (p. 146). We as educators need to focus on depth of understanding over breadth of coverage. We must have the courage to cover less and go more deeply into the material; covering the material should not come at the expense of student understanding. At an ever-increasing number of schools, communication and collaboration are important pieces of the curricular puzzle.

We as educators need to focus on depth of understanding over breadth of coverage.

At Sacramento New Technology High School in California, collaborating with peers and oral communication are part of the curriculum. Skills in these areas must be mastered in addition to traditional academic material (Gewertz, 2007, p. 25). Beverly Nelson (1996) teaches science in a New Jersey high school with students who represent more than 99 nationalities. Her biggest challenge is "persuading students of different backgrounds and cultures to work together" (Nelson, 1996, p. 22). To achieve this end, Nelson forms cooperative learning teams and creates new teams periodically. She recognizes that "students cannot be necessarily expected to function as a team" simply because they have been organized in teams (Nelson, 1996, p. 24). Understanding that being able to cooperate effectively is important for her students, she works hard at helping them acquire the basic skills needed to make teamwork the norm.

If students are indeed spending more and more of their own time in front of two-dimensional screens, then classrooms must become three-dimensional laboratories where students can acquire the skills they need to be successful. Structured conversation is an important part of that equation. Students who are petrified to talk in front of a group can begin to overcome that fear by working in pairs and then in small groups.

The Simultaneity Principle

I spent a good many years as a teacher having conversations with a mere handful of my students in any given class. The others were polite, for the most part, but they were not engaged in any meaningful way. Early in my career, I rarely had students work in pairs or in groups to discuss anything meaningful or to problem-solve or work collaboratively on meaningful projects or tasks. I spent a lot of time saying, "Do your own work, please!"

When teachers do most of the talking and when interactions are between a few students and the teacher, those students *not* involved in the conversation have tacit permission to disengage. Students who are not encouraged to communicate frequently will *not*, unsurprisingly perhaps, learn to communicate well. Because they are not engaged, they become bored. When students take part in paired or group discussions, they are involved and engaged in their own learning. According to Kagan (1994), when students are paired for conversations, half the class is talking, and when this happens, "There is 15 times as much student language production over subject matter" (p. 4:7). Kagan calls this the simultaneity principle.

Part of the problem with getting students to share, of course, is that speaking in front of a group of their assembled peers frightens many of them, even in the best of circumstances. Indeed, I know many adults who can teach all day long and enjoy it, yet are petrified of presenting at a faculty meeting or speaking to a group of parents at a PTA meeting. Much of that fear comes from the possibility that taking the risk of sharing will result in embarrassment. "Fear of physical harm and fear of embarrassment often have the same effect" (Rogers & Renard, 1999, p. 35). Teachers need to create the kind of safe environment in which students are not afraid to open up and risk failure in the form of embarrassment or humiliation.

There also may be anxiety on the part of students as to how the teacher or their peers will react to what they share with the class. If students are unclear about how a teacher or their classmates will respond, they may be less likely to take the risk that comes with sharing. According to Burke (2008), "Students do not feel free to engage in interactive discussion, contribute ideas, or share experiences if they are never sure when they will incur the teacher's wrath or become the object of the teacher's sarcasm or anger" (p. 85). If they feel safe, structures for conversation can be put in place on a regular basis. Tate (2003) adds, "When students are given the opportunity to brainstorm ideas without criticism, to discuss opinions, to debate controversial issues, and to answer questions at all levels of Bloom's taxonomy, wonderful things can happen that naturally improve comprehension and higher order thinking" (p. 1).

> *If students are unclear about how a teacher or their classmates will respond, they may be less likely to take the risk that comes with sharing.*

A student who may be afraid to communicate orally with the whole class may be willing to share with one other person with whom he feels comfortable. Any teacher who is putting students in pairs for the first time may want to consider carefully who is paired with whom. First things first, and the first thing is to get students talking with someone they know and trust *about something with which they are familiar.* The idea here is to get the *process* down while providing a formal structure to which they can become accustomed over time.

In her Terry High School (Texas) medical microbiology classroom, Elise Brune provides her students with multiple opportunities for paired and group discussions beginning early in the school year. The tables in Brune's classroom accommodate small groups of four or five students, and she frequently changes the seating assignments, something she has found "allows students to become more familiar and at ease around one another, leading to more participation and sharing of opinions and ideas" (personal email, 2/10/19). This collaborative groundwork pays dividends when Brune moves into more complicated material later on, including a lesson on the structure of viruses.

As students enter the classroom, they are randomly assigned to groups. "Each group is assigned a short reading about a specific structure found in a virus particle. They have a specific amount of time to read the description, identify the important pieces of information (with graphic organizers to help with this), and decide how to teach the important information to the next group" (personal email, 2/8/19). Each of Brune's students gets a chance to present part of this complex topic to classmates during the course of the lesson. It continues until all the virus structures have been covered by students in teaching mode.

The simultaneity principle should begin, as it does in Elise Brune's microbiology classroom over the course of the school year, with students working in pairs, then in small groups. Restructuring groups from time to time gets students used to working with—and having substantive academic conversations with—everyone in the classroom at one time or another. Brune develops a collaborative culture beginning with frequent structured conversations early on. She also spends a good deal of time getting to know—and building rapport with—her students. Success so often begins with the basics. In the world of structured conversations, the basics begin with pairs.

Working in Pairs

Assume for the moment that a teacher has spent a good deal of time at the beginning of the year establishing rapport, building positive relationships, embedding powerful and effective procedures and routines, and, in general, establishing a climate in which students will not mind sharing ideas with each other. Realizing that the next step in the transition to an interactive classroom may be providing a structure for students to communicate orally and openly, the teacher must make a decision about how that might be accomplished. My advice would be to begin by having students work in pairs.

There are at least four advantages of beginning the interactive journey with pairs, rather than larger groups of students:

1. A conversation with one other peer may be far less threatening than speaking in front of the whole class.

2. There is no place to hide in a pair. My experience has shown that, in a very large percentage of cases when students share in pairs, both partners contribute *something* to a given discussion. One partner may dominate, but we will look at ways to eliminate that later on.

3. The classroom can be set up so there is a permanent partner for each student. Prior to class, desks can be arranged so that the partners can have a conversation on cue, problem-solve in pairs, and help each other with difficult concepts.

4. Students who learn to work effectively and safely with a single partner will be less likely to resist the next step—the move to collaborative groups.

Before moving to content-laden paired discussions, students (most of whom may never have engaged in structured conversations of any sort with classmates), teachers can initiate paired conversations that concentrate on topics of a personal nature. This allows students to practice speaking and listening skills without having to worry about content just yet. The role of teachers during these conversations, and I recommend standing pairs, is to circulate, listen, and observe. At some point, the teacher will make the determination that students are ready for more academic-oriented conversations. Figure 3.1 lists some possible topics for paired conversations dealing with the personal.

As part of the process for any classroom conversation, the teacher will need a way to bring the students' attention back to her when she is ready to end the discussion. I use a signal that combines the visual and the auditory, no matter the age group. I hold my hand in the air and say, "Pause; look this way please. Finish your thought but not your paragraph." I explain that although I don't want the participants to cut off their discussion in midsyllable, I don't want them to continue for more than a few seconds. In other words, I want to honor the fact that I asked them to speak by permitting them to finish a thought or sentence before we move to the next activity. I have observed hundreds

First level (little thought required): their favorite . . .	Next level (more thought required):
• Television show • Movies • Books • Heroes • Vacation destinations • Cartoon characters • Food • Candy • Sports • Outdoor activities	• Way to build respect when working with other students or family members on a project • Favorite place and techniques to study for tests • Way to stay healthy and live a long life • Considerations families may have when deciding whether or not to move to another house, city, state or country

of teachers, trainers, presenters, and seminar facilitators over the years, and the most successful process managers are those who invest two minutes up front to establish this norm. It is cheap, but it pays great dividends immediately.

TTYPA (Turn to Your Partner and . . .)

Think about the process of lecturing for a moment. A teacher or professor stands up front and imparts information to students who are seated and taking notes. There are at least three things to consider from the vantage point of the student:

1. As the instructor talks, the student attempts simultaneously to listen and take notes without missing anything—no easy task under the best of circumstances.

2. While grappling with listening and taking notes, something the instructor just said happens to strike a responsive chord in the student's mind. He begins to ponder it while looking out the window. While he processes the information, he suddenly hears the instructor, in a change of pitch or tone, announce *point three*. The student muses, "What happened to *point two?*" The lecture is continuing apace, however, so he looks at someone else's notes to pick up on point two while missing point three . . . and

Tactical Tip

Empathy is an important component of friendships and working relationships. Consider having students, in standing pairs, discuss the following questions:

• What is the difference between empathy and sympathy?

• Why is empathy important to the development of working relationships and friendships?

• In what ways can we demonstrate empathy in our relationships?

• What role does empathy play in collaborative work in the classroom?

These discussions, along with whole-class conversations around empathy, should come early in the year, prior to the formation of groups and teams for project-based learning. Personal or professional stories from teachers can help students understand the role of empathy in the interactive classroom (or in the cafeteria, the gym, the hallway, or at the bus stop).

so on throughout what may be a lengthy lecture. There is no rewind button for the student in this situation.

3. All of this presupposes that there are no distractions during the lecture. Students may be arriving or leaving, the temperature may be uncomfortable, something may be going on outside the window, someone may be passing notes, a student with a cold may be coughing frequently . . . distractions can come in bunches, playing havoc with the whole process.

If we add to all this the fact that the average amount of time an adult can pay attention during a presentation is 15 minutes or less (and the attention span decreases as the age decreases), then the natural inclination to stop paying attention simply adds to the other difficulties I just listed (Allen, 2002, p. 31). The message here is that after 10 or, at the most, 15 minutes of lecturing, teachers and other presenters simply need to do something else. That something else can be as simple as saying, "Turn to your partner; take a moment to discuss point number one before moving on to point number two," or, "Turn to your partner and see if you agree with what the author says on page 22." Fogarty (1990) gives a convincing reason why TTYPA is so effective. "It is next to impossible to turn to your partner and . . . not say something. This simple strategy has a compelling ingredient in it. There is a built-in expectation for reciprocity. It's hard to drop out of a twosome when your partner is depending on you to complete the interaction" (p. 10).

> *Giving students some time to process the information the teacher just delivered will help them remember it.*

Giving students some time to process the information the teacher just delivered will help them remember it. Both partners may have received a different message from the same lecture segment. Talking about it may help them understand it a bit better or cause them to see if from the partner's perspective. As the teacher circulates around the room and listens to the various conversations, she will get an idea of how well they understand that 10 minutes' worth of information. If the students seem to be confused as they share, that may be an indication that the teacher needs to go back and work with the information a little more (and maybe from a different angle).

Modeling and Teaching Empathetic Listening

Whether these paired conversations succeed depends on students who are respectful of one another; student-to-student conversations can short-circuit quickly (and publicly) if students don't take the time to reflect on and try to understand what others are saying. This means pausing and thinking a bit before responding, and it requires patience and moments of reflective silence when working together with a partner or partners. It requires empathy: "Conversations can provide practice for students in thinking about what the partner needs, wants, values, and feels" (Zwiers & Crawford, 2011, p. 16). Costa (2008) maintains students who are successful listeners are "able to see through the diverse perspectives of others. They gently attend to another person, demonstrating their understanding of and empathy for an idea or feeling by paraphrasing it accurately, building upon it, clarifying it, or giving an example of it" (p. 33). Empathy means attending to someone other than ourselves as we seek to understand what they are saying or feeling at the time.

This requires that teachers—first and foremost—model this kind of reflective thought and empathetic listening with other adults in the building. Choosing any topic, the teacher and the other adult can go back and forth, modeling effective and empathetic listening, and then invite students to talk with each other in pairs about what they observed. Some posted prompts can guide their discussions: What did you notice about how we communicated just now? Did anything stand out as it relates to process? The teacher can walk around listening to the student conversations, and she can pick up on several things she would like brought out, asking those students if they would mind sharing particular points. This can lead to a general discussion about what empathy is, and how the lack of it can raise barriers to meaningful conversations and collaborative work.

From empathy to supportive body language, teachers can model good oral language skills and then work with students as they learn to collaborate ever more effectively during the school year. Students who learn to apply excellent speaking and listening skills are in a position to work more effectively as members of classroom teams. Ritchhart, Church, and Morrison (2011) cite a study of sixth graders working in groups to solve mathematical problems. The study "found that group success was far less dependent on the academic skills of the group than it was in the group's ability to listen and respond to one another's ideas." Interestingly, "In these groups, individual members did not just talk; they also listened and sought greater equality among all group members," something that allowed them to build on each other's ideas "and advance far beyond groups with academically more proficient students" (Ritchhart et al., p. 37). The use of good listening skills can help students collaborate in ways that build their confidence and improve outcomes. This skill set includes pausing and paraphrasing as students seek to understand when working in collaborative settings.

> *Students who learn to apply excellent speaking and listening skills are in a position to work more effectively as members of classroom teams.*

Beginning with appropriate eye contact (not staring; breaking eye contact as the listener every so often, then coming quickly back), list several common-sense attributes of effective listening you can model for—and practice with—your students:

1. Appropriate eye contact
2.
3.
4.
5.
6.
7.
8.
9.

Pausing and Paraphrasing

One of my favorite college professors taught political science. He would ask a question, listen without interruption to the explanation put forth by a student (these were not low-level questions), look off to the side for a few seconds, and paraphrase what the student said. If the student added a bit more, he would listen, turn as he paused, and then paraphrase again. To me it was wonderful. His pauses gave us all time to think (what a concept!), and his questions were more open than closed. He was not necessarily attempting to have us all converge on a single, correct answer. Everyone in his class had time to think and wrestle with the alligator. That professor listened as we had our say, paraphrased, and gave us more time to engage in the discussion. He modeled pausing and paraphrasing, and we did not consider his classes one-way information dumps. We were true participants in this process, and he demonstrated his respect for us by modeling these two components of active listening. Teachers can model pausing and paraphrasing constantly; there are countless opportunities to do this during whole-class discussions.

Zwiers and Crawford (2011) include paraphrasing as one of five core skills for academic conversations (the other four are elaborating and clarifying, supporting ideas with examples, building on and challenging a partner's idea, and synthesizing conversation points). The authors point out that paraphrasing, as well as the other core skills, doesn't come naturally. Following is a partial listing of what Zwiers and Crawford call *Frames for Prompting the Skill:*

- I'm not sure that was clear . . .

- What do we know so far?

- What is your take on what I said?

- I don't know. Did that make sense?

- What are you hearing?

Notice how the speaker in each case invites his partner(s) to jump in and help provide clarification; a few *Frames for Responding* follow:

- So, you are saying that . . .

- Let me see if I understand you . . .

- Essentially, you think that . . .

- It sounds like you are saying that . . .

Listeners can use these frames to let a partner or everyone involved in a larger discussion know this is what they are thinking concerning what has been said so far. To be able to do that, listeners must actually listen; they must process what is being said, and they must analyze and infer in order to paraphrase accurately.

When it comes to pausing and paraphrasing, teachers can take the lead in two ways: First, they can model these two skills as they work the room, listening to what students say during whole-class conversations. Second, listening skills in general should be part of a conversation at the small-group and whole-class levels. Students can help teachers develop a list of excellent listening skills, and those skills can be modeled by teachers and practiced by students. These are process skills and, as in any sport, require a great deal of coaching on the part of the teacher (and peers) and plenty of practice.

YOUR TURN

When the information flow in a classroom is from the teacher to selected students, others in the room do not have the opportunity to engage in the dialogue; in fact, most students may simply disengage entirely. In this way, over the years, students learn to live with passive behavior; they can turn it off when necessary; they can also let others in the classroom—the teacher most of all—carry the load. Structured conversations provide students with an opportunity to process information and develop communication skills, and this can *begin*, as we have seen, with students working in pairs.

As students talk with one another in these structured conversations, teachers can listen carefully while moving among the pairs. They can take mental notes about something they may want to raise or highlight when the activity is done. They can also ask students if they will share something later; this gives students who don't normally share in whole-class settings a chance to shine. These paired academic conversations will give students the oral language skills that will serve them well when they move into larger groups down the road.

REFLECTIVE QUESTIONS

Is your room configured to facilitate movement and standing pair shares? If not, what changes can you make?

Which among the conversation topics in Figure 3.1 do you think could be used in your classroom for seated or standing pairs?

What other topics, given the age of your students, might serve to get students started on the road to productive, content-related discussions? (Here are some others that might be considered second-level conversation topics: What is friendship? What can we learn from the perspectives of a friend? What is empathy? How can we demonstrate empathy in our conversations or interactions with others?)

How can you model the pause and the paraphrase for your students?

As you begin to plan your lessons—individually or with a colleague (or colleagues)—what decisions can be made in order to decrease the amount of teacher talk and increase the frequency of student-to-student conversations?

Managing Movement in the Classroom

Here is a thread that runs through a good many adult-centered classrooms, especially at the secondary level: Students seem to spend a good deal of time thinking of ways to get up from their seats and move around the room or into the hallways. A trip to the pencil sharpener becomes a necessity for a student whose pencil is probably sharp enough. A few minutes in the hall becomes the goal of a student who may not really need to go to the restroom. The trip itself is the real motivator because the alternative is to sit still for yet another extended period of time. I have seen teachers expend enormous amounts of energy trying to keep kids in their seats and quiet. Yet the most successful teachers I have observed and coached over the years don't fight this natural proclivity for movement on the part of students—they take advantage of it; *they harness it as an instructional tool.*

One of the basic tenets of brain-based learning is that movement facilitates the learning process (Blaydes, 2004; Dennison & Dennison, 1994; Sprenger, 2002; Wolfe, 2001). Jensen (2005a) makes the case that "movement can be an effective cognitive strategy to (1) strengthen learning, (2) improve memory and retrieval, and (3) enhance learner motivation and morale" (p. 60). Erlauer (2003) puts it this way: "Students who are required to stand or move around during a lesson have less physical fatigue and therefore concentrate more efficiently on the concepts or tasks at hand" (p. 46). In classrooms where movement is integrated into lessons on a regular basis, students appreciate the difference between this and other classes where movement is nowhere on the menu. Students who have to sit for a long time tend to seek mental destinations as welcome alternatives to a largely sedentary class period or block.

Classroom teachers who want students to display a great deal of energy can't simply will that energy into existence. Saying things like, "Pay attention now!" or, "Work with me here, people!" doesn't help. The brain needs something, and that something is not exhortations and waggling fingers from the front of the room. "The brain is an energy guzzler that imbibes roughly 20 percent of the body's energy," says Posey (2019), "so options to move, such as stretching, standing, walking, or playing, can increase oxygen intake and help keep the brain fueled with energy" (p. 60). I have seen teachers become entertainers in an attempt to *inspire* in order to keep their students from *expiring,* but no matter how entertaining they are, the kids are still in their seats. Sitting for long periods of time simply decreases the energy level of students.

My experience working with adults over the past 12 years is that the same principle applies to them. At the beginning of every workshop I facilitate, I ask this question: "How many of you go to a better place in your minds after 10 minutes during a three-hour night class?" Nearly every hand goes up, and I invite them to keep their hands up and look around the room at a veritable sea of hands. Humans aren't built to sit for long periods without their eyes glazing over and their minds wandering. Teachers working with students and workshop facilitators working with adults would do well to provide plenty of opportunities for movement and, while participants are standing, for structured conversations.

> *Humans aren't built to sit for long periods without their eyes glazing over and their minds wandering.*

One of the accommodations needed to encourage simultaneous conversation and frequent movement has to do with furniture arrangement.

Reimagine Classrooms With Movement in Mind

I taught in a half-dozen different classrooms in my teaching career, and in every one of those settings, the teacher's desk was front and center when I arrived. The student desks were in straight rows with everyone facing the front of the room. In every instance, I left all the furniture that way and discovered that lecture and an overhead projector fit very well into that room arrangement. This configuration (still standard in many secondary settings) is teacher centered, not student centered, and makes an interactive, high-energy classroom difficult to achieve.

There are two major problems with the traditional furniture arrangement shown in Figure 4.1. One relates to classroom discipline. When the desks are in neat rows and fill most of the room, it is difficult for the teacher to use a critical tool in managing students: proximity. This five-by-six configuration "produces *five impermeable barriers* between the left side of the room and the right side" (Jones, 2007, p. 38). The feet of many students in a crowded classroom may touch the desk in front of them, making movement difficult. A teacher who needs to respond immediately to a problem four or five rows away will usually have to go completely around the phalanx of desks to get there.

Figure 4.1   Traditional Room Arrangement

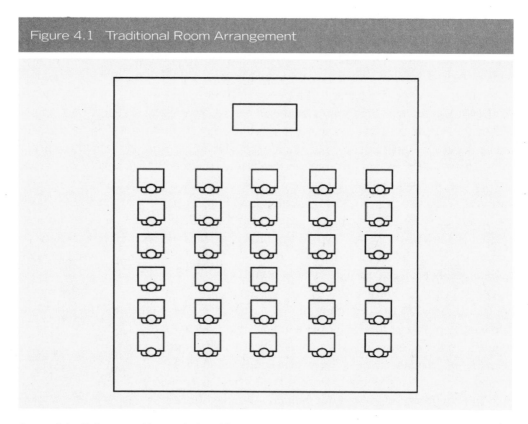

Source: Brian T. Jones, used by permission of Frederic H. Jones & Associates, Inc.

If this room arrangement creates mobility problems for the instructor, it also means if students are going to move about the room to meet and discuss something, they may bump into each other and the furniture as they try to get to the outside perimeters of the classroom. If you then ask them to find a *new* partner, movement once again will be confined to the perimeter. With a limited amount of space and with student desks filling the center of the room, movement becomes problematic.

To facilitate movement, teachers are advised to get the teacher's desk, typically front and center, out of the way (banishing it to a corner or to the back of the room). This opens up space in the front of the room. Jones (2007) suggests an arrangement like the one in Figure 4.2, one that contains an "interior loop with ears," to allow the teacher greater freedom of movement. It has the advantage of putting students in pairs to facilitate interaction. In a highly active classroom, this configuration gives everyone more space to maneuver and meet during paired or group activities.

One effective way to create more space is to move the student desks completely to the outside, opening up the entire center of the room for movement and structured conversations. This perimeter furniture arrangement allows a great deal of flexibility in terms of student and teacher movement.

Take a close look at Figures 4.2 and 4.3. Notice how the students in both configurations are in pairs or in groups of four. Space is created by pushing desks together. Not only does this allow the teacher more mobility; it also allows students more room in which to meet and process information, and the routes to get to those open spaces are shorter. The teacher can have students share with the person next to them or with the

---

Figure 4.2 "Interior Loop With Ears" Room Arrangement

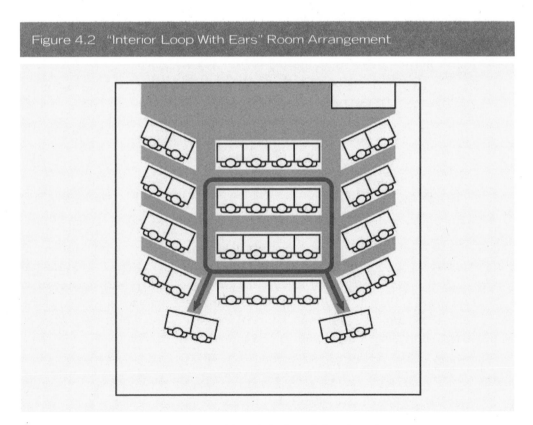

Source: Brian T. Jones, used by permission of Frederic H. Jones & Associates, Inc.

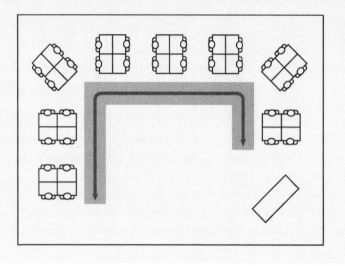

Figure 4.3 Perimeter Room Arrangement

Source: Brian T. Jones.

Tactical Tip

Getting students into pairs can be a chore, a disaster, or seemingly effortless. Students not used to standing, pairing, and sharing in a highly interactive environment need to spend a good deal of time practicing getting from their seats into standing pairs. I suggest using some upbeat music to accompany the move. That song should be used only for this purpose, getting them to and from their desks. The time limit for accomplishing the move should be clearly defined and held to by the teacher. Students will take all the time they want to take if we let them. Perfect execution requires perfect practice.

person across from them, or the *entire group* of four can communicate on some topic on request. In Figure 4.3, the entire center of the room is opened up so students can stand, meet, and move.

If we accept, then, that students need to move and attending to room arrangement is a necessary and important precursor to that movement, we can explore some suggestions of just how to use that movement to help class or seminar participants process information on their feet. Each of the following strategies involves a structured conversation that allows students to verbalize points of view, summarize information, compare answers, gain new insights, and process new information.

In Chapter 3, we introduced strategies for conversations or brainstorming with students in their normal classroom seating arrangement. The following strategies ask students to stand and move about the room to meet with someone not in their original table group. Meeting with students outside their own closely knit groups may be uncomfortable at first, but part of developing communication skills involves moving outside this familiar circle of friends.

In Melissa Martini's fifth-grade classroom at Sanders Corner Elementary School (Virginia), students have their pick from among various chairs, stools, exercise balls, and other seating options. Notice in Figure 4.4, Martini's students also have their choice of desk surfaces of various sizes, styles, and height. iGen'ers like choice, and flexible configurations like this honor that reality.

Figure 4.4 Melissa Martini's Flexible Room Configuration

Source: Photo by Melissa Martini.

Here are questions students can discuss in standing pairs:

- Why is exercise beneficial to the human body?

- In what ways does the ability to move about in the classroom benefit you and your classmates?

- How can you ensure transitions are conducted safely and quickly in this classroom?

Getting Both Partners Involved

One problem associated with paired discussions is that one student may dominate the conversation, leaving his partner in the proverbial dust for the time allotted by the teacher. The dominant student continues to build his communication skills while his partner is relegated to a minor and not very interesting role in the proceedings. One way to ensure both students have a chance to contribute is to give these instructions:

- "I'm going to give you 60 seconds to complete this conversation. I don't care which partner begins. Decide now who will begin." (wait)

- "About 30 or so seconds into this, I want the partner who started the conversation to use his or her partner's name, saying, 'What do you think, John?' Remember, use your partner's name, and invite him or her into the conversation. I'll take care of the 60 seconds; you take care of your partner."

- "Questions? (wait) You have about 60 seconds. Go."

- At or near the end of the time allotted, the instructions would sound like this:

- "Finish your thought. [pause] Please thank your partner for sharing. Turn and face me." (Wait until everyone is facing you in silence before doing anything else. If you talk while someone is still talking, you give them permission to talk over you every time you do this.)

A teacher who has asked students to talk with each other in standing pairs should allow them to finish a thought and not stop in midsentence or syllable. A short pause should give them time to wrap things up.

During the first week of school, students can practice simple conversations (favorite foods, movies, vacation destinations) while making sure to bring the other person into the discussion about halfway through—always using that person's name. This provides a bit of structure and keeps one person from dominating the proceedings. Content-laden conversations can wait, frankly, until students get the process down. Summarization, asking questions to provide clarity, and anything more difficult than talking respectfully with a partner can wait as well; my experience is that many students have had few, if any, chances to discuss something with someone other than the teacher in a structured way. The whole idea of standing, facing a classmate, and *attending to that person* is something that needs to be practiced until it becomes second nature.

> The whole idea of standing, facing a classmate, and attending to that person is something that needs to be practiced until it becomes second nature.

Paired Verbal Fluency (PVF)

The next step is a much more formal and structured strategy called paired verbal fluency (PVF). As with the structure before, PVF (Lipton & Wellman, 2000) ensures both partners get a chance to share and begins with the establishment of learning partners and a quick decision as to who will be Partner A and who will be Partner B. The teacher assigns a topic to be discussed and then has A or B go first.

Teachers will want to explain that *attentive listening* involves facing the partner directly, establishing good eye contact, and using positive body language. Over the years, I have worked with middle school students on facilitating groups. The whole concept of making eye contact and paying attention to body language is something I found we had to work on extensively before we could do anything else. If the listener in a pair is partner A and his or her body language is negative or demonstrates indifference (Figure 4.5), the conversation will never get off the ground.

Figure 4.5   Indifferent Posture

Figure 4.6   Supportive Posture

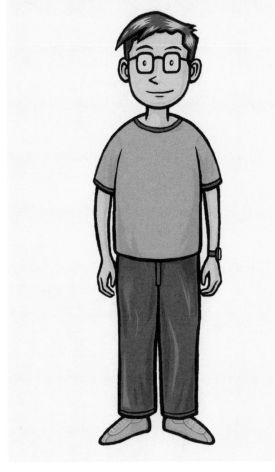

Source: Brian T. Jones.

Source: Brian T. Jones.

Figure 4.6 shows a supportive posture that students can use when they are in the role of listener. Note that the feet are slightly apart. The smile is intended to encourage the listener's partner. Most importantly, there are no distractions for the speaker (smirks, scowls, arm waving, hands in pockets, extravagant gestures, slouching, or sighing). Students have enough difficulty focusing and conversing without the additional obstacles that negative body language and facial expressions can create.

Getting students to adopt a supportive posture like that in Figure 4.6 is only half the battle, however. The student who is in the role of the listener has to, well, *listen.* According to Costa (2008), we often "say we are listening, but in reality we are rehearsing in our head what we are going to say next when our partner is finished" (p. 33). Moreover, according to Costa (2008), "We wish students

Tactical Tip

Every time students are in standing pairs, take the time to introduce a listening skill they can discuss (supportive body language, appropriate eye contact, not interrupting) and use. I watched a second-grade class use PVF effectively, and the teacher told me they worked hard on their listening skills, something that was obvious by the way her students handled themselves in action. A great time to introduce them and talk about them is while they are in standing pairs; after all, this is where they will most often use the skills until they shift into small groups later on.

to hold in abeyance their own values, judgments, opinions, and prejudices in order to listen to and entertain another person's thoughts" (p. 33). This is difficult for students even in the best of circumstances. Keeping one's body language neutral and supportive is difficult, to be sure, but it is necessary if students are going to engage in conversations and process information in pairs or groups. Teachers need to take the time *to talk about and model* supportive listening for students as they work to develop their own conversational skills.

As you will see in the step-by-step approach to PVF in Figures 4.7 and 4.8, it is often necessary for students to summarize what a partner has just said *or* continue a discussion on the same topic without repeating what the partner communicated a minute or so earlier. The listener can't simply mentally disconnect, nod, smile, and go somewhere else in his mind. If Partner A goes first, Partner B must listen carefully because his contribution to the conversation is dependent largely on what A already shared. Partner B will have to summarize or add to what A contributed to the conversation; listening carefully, respectfully, and supportively is therefore essential.

When using PVF, teachers should give one direction at a time whenever possible. Figure 4.7 outlines one possibility for the use of PVF. I strongly encourage that this be

Figure 4.7   PVF as a Step-By-Step Activity, With Directions

Note: Give the directions one at a time.
Direction: "Stand up, and find a partner other than someone at your table."
Direction: "Decide who will be A and who will be B."
Direction: "A, raise your hand." And **"B,** raise your hand." (then) "Hands down."
Direction: "Our topic for discussion is _____. **A,** when I say 'GO!' I'll give you 60 seconds to talk about the topic. Now **B,** while **A** is talking, listen carefully. When I say Switch! **B** will begin talking about this same topic with a twist. You may not repeat anything **A** said during his 60 seconds of fame."
Direction: "Look at the board once again to see the topic."
Direction: "A, you are on . . . GO!"
Partner **A** speaks directly to Partner **B** for 60 seconds on the chosen topic.
Direction: After 60 seconds, the teacher says, "Switch!"
On the same topic, Partner **B** takes over for 60 seconds, without repeating what **A** said.
Direction: After 60 seconds, the teacher says, "Stop! Look this way."
Direction: "Well done. Thank your partner for sharing. On to the next step."
Direction: 'This time, **B** will go first. As you think about the 2-minute conversation you and **A** had a few moments ago, were there some things left undiscussed, something important left out? When I say 'GO!' you'll have 30 seconds to add whatever you think has yet to be discussed as it relates to the topic. When I say 'Switch!' **A** will have another 30 seconds to add whatever he thinks has not been disclosed about the topic."
Direction: "B, you are on . . . GO!"

On the same topic, Partner B goes first and adds whatever he thinks might have been left out of the initial conversation.
Direction: After 30 seconds, the teacher says, "Switch!"
On the same topic, Partner **A** adds information he thinks was left unsaid so far in the conversation.
Direction: After 30 seconds, the teacher says, "Stop! Look this way."
Direction: "One final task, and **A** will go first. When I say 'GO!' **A** will summarize in 20 seconds or so some of the most important points made by both of you during the conversation. When I say 'Switch!' **B** will have the opportunity to summarize any points not made by A in a final 20 seconds. Questions?"
Direction: "**A,** you are on . . . GO!"
Partner **A** summarizes what was said so far.
Direction: After 20 seconds the teacher says, "Switch!"
Partner **B** adds to the summary what **A** may have left out.
Direction: After 20 seconds, the teacher says, "Stop! Look this way."
Direction: "Thank your partner **for** sharing, and take your seats!"

done with the students standing up, which is why I included it in the chapter on movement. I have found that if students are standing and facing each other, there are fewer distractions than if students are sitting at their desks. In fact, facing each other from across two typical student desks (and across piles of paper, books, laptops, etc.) can be awkward. Standing in an open area free of clutter allows both students to face each other and share in normal conversational tones. If teachers decide to have them switch partners during the activity, they are already on their feet and can move quickly to engage someone else in the class.

Figure 4.8 is another variation, again requiring strong listening and summarization skills on the part of both students. In this case, 60 seconds of conversation on the part of one partner is directly followed by a 30-second summary by the other. The roles are then reversed for the final phase.

Over the years, I have found PVF a powerful way for students to process new information just presented in a minilecture or to summarize something they have been studying for a few days. One key to success here is for the teacher to move around the room listening to the various conversations. By doing this, the teacher can determine if at the end of the first 2 minutes there is any need to go on to the second and third stages. Students who know the teacher is constantly moving and listening are far more likely to discuss that which the teacher desires to have discussed, rather than talking about Friday night's homecoming game or dance. Listening to students who are standing, I have discovered, is much easier than bending over repeatedly to pick up on conversations between or among students who are seated. If there is a written activity as a follow-up to PVF, the students will have been standing for long enough to make sitting down a nice change of pace.

One key to success with PVF is to make certain that the topic is broad or open enough to allow for a good deal of discussion. Also, teachers need to listen carefully for a decrease

Figure 4.8   A Shorter PVF as a Step-by-Step Activity, With Directions

Note: Give the directions one at a time.
Direction: "Stand up and find a partner other than someone at your table."
Direction: "Decide who will be **A** and who will be **B**."
Direction: "**A,** raise your hand." And "**B,** raise your hand." (then) "Hands down!"
Direction: "Our topic for discussion is _____. **A,** when I say 'GO!' I'll give you 60 seconds to talk about the topic. Now **B,** while A is talking, listen carefully. When I say 'Switch!' **B** will summarize what **A** said. In order to be able to do that effectively, you must listen carefully while **A** is speaking."
Direction: "Look at the board once again to see the topic."
Direction: "**A,** you are on . . . GO!"
Partner **A** speaks directly to Partner **B** for 60 seconds on the chosen topic.
Direction: After 60 seconds, the teacher says, "Switch!"
Partner **B** summarized what **A** said.
Direction: After 60 seconds, the teacher says, "Stop! Look this way."
Direction: "Well done. Thank your partner for sharing. On to the next step."
Direction: "This time, **B** will go first. As you think about the 2-minute conversation you and **A** had a few moments ago, were there some things left undiscussed, something important left out? When I say 'GO!' you'll have 60 seconds to add whatever you think has yet to be discussed as it relates to the topic. When I say 'Switch!' **A** will have 30 seconds to summarize what you said."
Direction: "**B,** you are on . . . GO!"
On the same topic, Partner **B** goes first and adds whatever he thinks might have been left out of the initial conversation.
Direction: After 60 seconds, the teacher says, "Switch!"
Partner **A** summarizes what **B** said.
Direction: After 30 seconds, the teacher says, "Pause . . . and look this way!"
Direction: "Thank your partner **for** sharing, and take your seats!"

Here are a few more questions students can discuss in standing pairs:

- What benefits do you receive from working with a partner or partners?

- What kinds of body language support a partner or the other members of a team?

- Why is using the names of your classmates when you are collaborating so important?

- In what ways can you indicate to your partner you are actively listening?

in volume or body language that shows students are winding down their conversations, especially during the 60-second segments. Sixty seconds is a long time, and teachers need to make some adjustments, if necessary, based on what they hear or see during the discussions. There is no need to drag out to a full minute a conversation that is obviously winding down.

Gallery Walks

One of our favorite destinations is the National Gallery of Art in the nation's capital. Having gained admittance, normally as soon as they open, I head immediately for the 19th-century American art section of the museum, then make a beeline for my favorite oil painting: Winslow Homer's *Breezing Up* (*A Fair Wind*). On my last trip to the National Gallery, I watched from a bench as an artist worked on his own version of that famous painting; we engaged in a conversation about Homer in general and about that oil painting in particular. He saw things I did not see, and those several minutes helped me understand much about my favorite artist and his work. The conversation was as instructive as it was enjoyable. I typically spend several hours in what amounts to an extensive gallery walk—in an incredible gallery of art in our nation's capital.

Gallery walks need not be limited to art museums. Over the years, I have seen teachers at all grade levels and subject areas use this strategy to get students up, moving, thinking, sharing, explaining, and learning. After lunch in one first-grade classroom, I watched as students paired up at pieces of student art displayed around the room, using markers and sticky notes to write descriptive words they then placed next to a particular piece of art. When the music started, the pairs moved in turn to the next station; this continued until each pair was back where they had begun. This was a great way for these first graders to expand their use of descriptors (including colors) while on their feet, working with partners. From my vantage point in the center of the classroom, I noticed that they had some great conversations, too.

Diana Abil-Mona, a seventh-grade science teacher at George Junior High School (Texas), understands that she is not the only teacher in the room, and she frequently uses the gallery walk in her classes to encourage discussions on various topics between and among students in groups no larger than four. For example, each year, Abil-Mona creates several stations around her science classroom, each representing a specific biome (a community of plants and animals inhabiting a distinct region). In a timed gallery walk (5 minutes at each station), small groups of students move from one station to another, discussing what they see and dealing with questions related to each biome. Abil-Mona's job is to "walk around the classroom and monitor discussions," asking questions based on the discussions. These frequent gallery walks allow her students "to take ownership of their own learning" (personal email, 2/10/19).

One of the great things about gallery walks is that it gives the teacher a 360-degree view of the proceedings. In the example, Abil-Mona is able to listen in on the conversations and ask questions when appropriate. Most of all, she gets an idea of where her students are in their understanding of a particular topic or concept. This provides valuable feedback for her as she decides where to go next; in this way, the information gleaned from the gallery walk informs her instruction. It also provides her students with multiple opportunities to explain, describe, illustrate, and ask questions of each other along the way. Talking is thinking; thinking is learning.

YOUR TURN

Movement provides a change of pace for students and enhances the learning process. Students experience three distinct phases of movement during all three of the strategies introduced in this chapter: (1) standing and forming a pair or small group, (2) sharing with the partner(s), and (3) finding their way back to their seats. Classrooms can be configured so that transitions and activities that require movement can be completed safely and quickly.

REFLECTIVE QUESTIONS

Before you incorporate movement and standing pair shares (or any other collaborative structures) into your daily routine, will the physical classroom configuration support it? (A rule of thumb is the same one I use when cleaning my office or closet a couple of times a year—if I don't use it or wear it, I give it away. I once worked with a middle school teacher to remove furniture, books, and anything else that wasn't really needed from the room. Then, we rearranged what was left to facilitate the movement and interactions of pairs and groups.)

Is there a colleague in your hallway or your building who uses movement and standing pair shares frequently? (If so, observing her classroom might provide some ideas for you. It may also be that there is a teacher in another school in the district whom you could observe and with whom you could have a conversation when the observation is over.)

If you don't regularly incorporate movement into your classroom routine, which one of the activities in this chapter could you use with your course content?

If you use movement and two or three academic-conversation strategies from Monday through Thursday, what kind of feedback mechanism could you use on Friday to solicit feedback from your students concerning its effectiveness?

CHAPTER 5

Presenting With Confidence

Several years ago, I observed a workshop facilitator who used an overhead projector for 3 hours, reading from the transparencies as they appeared on the screen. After the break (much appreciated by the audience), the facilitator fired up the projector once again and paused expectantly, waiting for the participants to stop talking and seat themselves so the session could resume. Nothing happened; people simply continued socializing well past the appointed resumption time. Finally, the facilitator began to say things like "Okay . . . if we could all be seated . . . please turn to page six in your handout . . . " This was all said quietly and hesitantly, as if she simply did not want to bother anyone.

Slowly, at the speed of a long freight train clearing a crossing, participants began to respond and, within a couple of minutes, return to their seats. It was painful to watch. Actually, the presenter had much worthwhile information to impart, and there were a few opportunities for members of the audience to interact. But her presentation and group facilitation skills were lacking, a reality that adversely affected the session and blunted its message and intended outcomes. The subsequent evaluations reflected the dissatisfaction of a high percentage of those who attended. They felt their time was precious and their needs as learners were not being met.

This conference session was for adults who *chose* to attend, and a few departed at the break or during the second part of the session. Unfortunately, students don't have the luxury of being able to vote with their feet. School attendance is compulsory, and any skill deficit on the part of a teacher is just bad luck for students . . . and something to be endured. "We will endure!" is hardly a stirring rallying cry for students who would much rather participate in their own learning than sit passively until their eyes glaze over and the daydreaming begins.

Content is critically important to teaching and learning, of course. It is, as Allen (2002) says, the reason we are all there. As he reminds us, however, *we teach people*, not content, whether we are working with students in a school or college setting or with adults in a seminar:

> The critical issue is that if the needs of the people in the group are interfering
> with learning the content at a particular time, then the quality of subsequent
> instruction is greatly reduced. Responding immediately to the requirements of
> a group, or an individual, will allow for enhanced concentration on the part
> of participants. All learners are people first, and adapting to meet their needs
> respects them as unique individuals. (p. 13)

In planning the seminar I described at the beginning of this chapter, our facilitator did not take into account the physical and mental needs of the audience; she had no single way of bringing everyone back after the break or when she had them talk in groups; she used the overhead projector as a crutch for the better part of 3 hours. It was mostly a one-way information flow. We were attendees—not participants. As I have related in every one of my books and presentations, attendees attend, and, to be fair, they may learn something. *Participants* learn a great deal more, and they hold on to it longer.

Presenters and Facilitators

In monologic classrooms dominated by teacher talk, teachers often assign themselves the role of lead (or only) presenter. The rest of the cast, in the form of students, may be resigned to their roles as mulling villagers or bit players, with no speaking role. My experience is that a presenter has about 10 (or fewer) minutes before the audience comes to the conclusion that this seminar, class period, block, or conference session is going to be an information dump that is both familiar and uninspiring. Sitting off to the side of the session I described, I quickly came to the conclusion that things might not end well. Things didn't, and this is often the case in classrooms.

When designing the classroom experience, it is best if teachers make sure students have their turn at presenting to each other and/or to the whole class at some point. Building communication skills requires practice; there are no shortcuts here. This is particularly true in project-based-learning settings, where students are required to make presentations to the class, the school board, community groups, or to other classes or student groups. They may present their findings at various stages during their work, using data and visuals created along the way. This presents a challenge for a teacher used to a traditional, adult-centered approach. "Rather than serving as information providers," affirms Bender (2012), "PBL requires teachers to serve as facilitators and instructional coaches, as students move through their project activities" (p. 39). Facilitating process for myriad projects may well require more energy and flexibility on the part of teachers unfamiliar with—and anxious about—an entirely interactive approach to learning.

Facilitating process for myriad projects may well require more energy and flexibility on the part of teachers unfamiliar with—and anxious about—an entirely interactive approach to learning.

Garmston and Wellman (1992) ask teachers to consider what they value as they work on the presentation components of lesson design. "If you value classrooms as learning communities in which students are interactive learners invested in each other's success, these values will permeate your presentation design and processes" (p. 3). The best teachers I have observed over the years model good presentation skills and get their students involved in developing and practicing those skills. Students who sit, watch, and pretend to listen are not going to leave classrooms and schools with any confidence when it comes to presenting or otherwise communicating face to face with peers or adults.

Rapport, Relationships, and Rehearsals

Presenters at conferences generally don't have time to develop deep and lasting relationships with audiences. The best among them use some humor and a story up front to make an emotional connection with fellow educators. For me as a presenter, this connection makes it far easier to turn attendees into participants a few minutes into the session. I want them up, moving, pairing, sharing, laughing, and learning; establishing even a limited rapport with an audience helps in facilitating a highly interactive and fast-paced session where participants are not afraid to engage.

When a speaker tells no stories, uses no humor, and makes no attempt to connect emotionally with an audience, the results can be less than satisfactory for the presenter and the audience. I watched from the back of an auditorium as a speaker who started late read from the pages in a binder, turning the pages and glancing at his watch as he read. He kept saying he needed to get to the airport. I wanted to volunteer to take him to the airport right then, sparing the audience further pain. Great presenters—and great teachers—work to bond emotionally with everyone in the room. Along the way, presenters and teachers-as-presenters become facilitators of process as the presentation venue or classroom becomes more and more interactive. I have seen presenters build an incredible amount of rapport in a conference session lasting only 90 minutes. In a full-day or multiday session, a good presenter/facilitator will invariably learn—and frequently use—the names of many or, in a small group, all of the participants. The same is true in classrooms.

The first step in building a relationship is to use someone's name—and pronounce it correctly. If I am looking at a name tag and remain unsure as to how to pronounce the name printed on it, I'll make sure of the pronunciation before attempting to use the name. Elementary teachers who want to build rapport on the way to building personal and working relationships with students should memorize everyone's name before lunch on the first day of school, having students cover their name tags or turn over their name cards as she walks around the room and correctly pronounces each name. Names are important to people. Taking the time and making the effort to learn them will set you aside as someone who wants to get to know them as human beings.

> *The first step in building a relationship is to use someone's name—and pronounce it correctly.*

It is important that teachers not only establish teacher–student relationships early but work toward developing solid working relationships between and among students right out of the gate. I have yet to see a highly interactive and synergistic classroom where students were not both congenial and collegial. A central-office colleague and I interviewed a classroom of fifth graders who let us know they had become a family over the course of the school year. I observed that particular classroom many times, and those kids were as consistently interactive as any I have seen. They worked efficiently in pairs and groups, performed plays, sang, danced, laughed frequently, took care of each other, *and aced the standardized tests at the end of the year*. Building effective relationships was job one for the two teachers who worked with those kids every day.

As mentioned in Chapter 3, if we want students to collaborate productively and efficiently down the road or present in a whole-class format or in front of an adult audience, the best place to start is with pairs. Get them used to communicating face to face with each other before moving them into teams where they will need to present the results of a project to others. Students will be much less anxious if they can practice their team presentations in what Boss and Larmer (2018) call low-risk situations. "You might start by having each team present to another team or record themselves on video and do a self-critique" (p. 147). I had occasion to observe as a team of eighth graders rehearsed a presentation they were scheduled to give to the school board, offering up their own feedback and receiving suggestions from the teachers who were working with them on the project.

The teachers who facilitated those eighth-grade groups worked with their students on presentation skills regularly while students worked on project content. Students who

Tactical Tip

Be conscious of the fact that students who are going to be asked to make presentations as part of their involvement in project-based learning will look to you to model excellent presentation skills. Two such skills involve making frequent eye contact and using the names of students frequently. I have observed classrooms where the teacher spends a good deal of time writing on—and looking at—a whiteboard, making little or no eye contact at all. Students left out of the learning process can be excused if they feel left out of the learning process. In presentation mode, teachers utilize both of these presentation/facilitation skills—eye contact and the frequent use of student names (properly pronounced)—to their advantage and to the satisfaction of their students.

are expected to present individually or in teams can learn to work seamlessly when it comes to a public presentation. And those skills matter. "As a project progresses," assert Boss and Larmer, "most of the teacher's and students' energy is focused on completing products and arriving at an answer to the driving question. But when it's time for students to share their work with an audience, poor presentations can seriously detract from the experience" (p. 149). Presentation skills do not simply appear when needed; they must be taught and practiced until they are second nature for students—and teachers.

> *Presentation skills do not simply appear when needed; they must be taught and practiced until they are second nature for students—and teachers.*

The teacher-as-presenter works alone, but students working on projects in teams must learn to present as a team. Athletic coaches spend a great deal of time on basic skills, but the mark of a great team is the capacity for working together. Michael Jordan famously said that talent can win games, but teamwork wins championships. Let's look at some basic presentation skills that can serve teachers and students well. Along the way, we'll look at ways to help students work as teams as they present to any audience.

Purposeful Movement

One of my college professors stood at the lectern, lit a cigarette, and proceeded to read from a set of yellowing notes in a grayish voice. I can't honestly say he ever moved once he hit his mark behind the lectern and lit his first cigarette of the morning. This lack of movement, combined with a lack of enthusiasm and the mother of all monotone voices served to make us glance frequently at our watches, willing the time to move more quickly. Conversely, I have seen presenters move entirely *too* much on occasion, and that can become a distraction for an audience. I discovered I was guilty of that when a participant pointed it out to me during a workshop, and I have worked on this ever since. The key is to move, stop moving, then move again with purpose, while keeping one's gestures under control.

Hoff (1992) has given presenters three great reasons to move around a presentation venue or classroom:

1. The audience is more likely to pay attention if the presenter is not glued to one spot. Their eyes (and heads) will follow the movement of the presenter. According to Hoff, "Since physiologists tell us that 80 percent of all human motivation is optically stimulated, you'd be silly not to give [the eyes of the audience members] a little workout." (p. 85)

2. Movement reduces stress on the part of the presenter.

3. Proximity is a great management tool, and moving among the audience "gives everybody a feeling of participation." (p. 85)

Movement with purpose includes the use of proximity, that is, moving closer to or away from a student. Once a student begins to answer a question, the teacher can *move away* from the student. Increasing the distance between teacher and student forces the student to speak more loudly (Smith, 2004), and this allows the teacher to observe and monitor the rest of the class in the process. So moving *in* causes a student to speak more softly and moving *away* has the opposite effect; if the teacher is standing right in front of a student, there is no need for the student to speak up.

Many teachers identify locations in the room that serve specific functions when they are in presentation mode. For example, Grinder (2000) points out that given the fact that "80% of communication is nonverbal, the need to control the microphone can be done by having two locations: one for the presentation and the other for handling/encouraging questions" (p. 176). A teacher may present some information in lecture mode from a specific position in the classroom. To make it clear to the students when they will be able to ask questions, he may then actually move a few steps away to a *second location* in the room and take those questions. After using this strategy several times, it would no longer be necessary to actually *ask* for questions. The fact that the teacher has moved to that position in the room is enough to indicate that the floor is open for students who have comments or questions.

Many classrooms still contain lecterns, and I can remember observing classrooms in my role as social studies coordinator where teachers held tightly to the lectern in ways reminiscent of Linus clutching his security blanket. Hoff reminds us that lecterns "put obstacles between you and your audience when you should be doing everything in your power to clear all obstacles away" (p. 81). Moving behind a lectern may signal the approach of a lengthy lecture, causing students to slide toward disengagement. Get rid of the temptation by getting rid of the lectern.

Moving behind a lectern may signal the approach of a lengthy lecture, causing students to slide toward disengagement. Get rid of the temptation by getting rid of the lectern.

When in listening mode, after a student asks a question or shares something in a whole-class setting, teachers as presenters can stop moving and face the student. Rather than staring at the student, however, the teacher can look away into the middle distance briefly, then make eye contact again, nodding and otherwise displaying supportive body language. I watched a teacher pace back and forth while a high school student was trying to explain something, and the *visual* (the teacher moving back and forth) played havoc with the *explanation*, so that I did not hear what the student was saying. I suspect I was not the only one in the room for whom that was a problem. In a struggle between the visual and the verbal, the visual wins.

If a member of the presentation team wishes to add something to what was already said by a teammate, rather than waving your hand or saying, "I can add something to that!" simply move quietly and smoothly a few feet away from the current presenter (in line with him) and stand quietly until he is finished. This indicates to him that you have something to add, and he can move to the side of the presentation area while you talk. If you know he has more to say, you can simply move back to where you were to begin with, and he can move up front and take your place. I have seen this done most effectively, and it allows a teammate to contribute something important while not causing confusion. It is smooth, quiet, efficient, and effective.

Here are some questions related to presenting that students can discuss in standing pairs:

- How does movement on the part of a presenter affect your concentration as a listener?

- When working with a team, why is it important to stay still, quiet, and, if possible, out of sight while one member of the team is in presentation mode?

- What effect does standing behind a lectern have on listeners?

- When in speaking mode, how can gestures support your message? At what point do gestures work against your message?

For many reasons, then, purposeful and deliberate movement on the part of the teacher—or student—as presenter is a useful tool. All this can be accomplished more effectively if some thought is given to room arrangement. According to Jones (2007), "The most important feature of room arrangement is *not* where the furniture goes, but, rather, where the furniture *does not go*. The objective of room arrangement is to create *walkways* in order to make mobility easy. I do not mean little, narrow walkways, I mean *boulevards*" (p. 41). When I am setting up for a workshop, I try to free up as much space for movement (mine and the workshop participants) as possible. In a presentation venue or a classroom, furniture should not serve as a detriment to the interactive nature of the learning experience.

Visuals and Technology

In Philadelphia many years ago, I had the opportunity to attend the seminar of a master presenter who used visuals to great effect. In an age when electronic presentations and colorful graphics predominate, this presenter used a black magic marker and white chart paper to perfection. Each of the charts he created (with our input) served as visual anchors for session participants, and the presenter returned to them repeatedly to reinforce concepts and information from earlier in the seminar. Unlike some slide presentations where the images pass in review and are gone, these simple, strong visuals allowed presenter and audience alike to visit them time and again during the seminar. These were simple visuals in the hands of someone who knew how to get the most from them—and from us.

The most powerful and effective teachers and presenters I know understand the impact of visuals. When visuals are created and then posted, students and seminar participants can use them to trigger thoughts and stimulate the thinking process. In fact, visual imagery connects with students "even when no reference is made to them in discussion" (Dickinson, 1995, p. 263). When the presenter or teacher as presenter allows time for seminar participants or students to contemplate and understand visuals, the images have more impact.

The key to using technology may be to understand that it supports the lesson but should not, as is often the case with slide presentations, *become* the lesson. Perhaps the most overused piece of technology available today, "the PowerPoint presentation is a small part of the whole instructional package" (de Wet, 2006, p. 6). The *whole* instructional/visual package may include the use of charts, graphs, overhead transparencies, artwork, student drawings and posters, markers, maps, traditional and electronic whiteboards, online learning platforms, laptops, tablet computers, and cell phones. These are all tools, of course, and should be seen as such. Success comes from knowing how to incorporate the technology into the lesson for maximum impact. That wonderful presenter in Philadelphia years ago used simple white charts and black markers as effectively as anything I have observed over the years.

Tactical Tip

When moving from one location to another in your classroom, avoid talking until you reach your destination. If, for example, you stood to the side as your students read some copy on the screen, you may want to get rid of the image on the screen, then move to the power position (front and center) to emphasize something. Wait until you arrive, face the students, smile, wait for everyone to stop talking or fidgeting, then say what you need to say. Any movement while you are talking causes a distraction and takes away from the verbal message. Visual beats auditory every time.

When the presenter or teacher as presenter allows time for seminar participants or students to contemplate and understand visuals, the images have more impact.

Visuals and technology, properly used, provide impact. Visuals provide clarification as well. Something described verbally in a classroom of 30 students may result in 30 different interpretations in the minds of those students. Adding the visual to the verbal clarifies thoughts and brings everything into focus. Leonardo da Vinci's notebooks are filled with about 1,500 drawings that illuminate and add visual clarity to his verbal descriptions of everything from flying machines to anatomical renderings of animals and humans (M. White, 2000). This has provided later generations—and not a few biographers—with a treasure trove of permanent visual images. Classroom teachers who complement the auditory with the visual can provide that same kind of impact, focus, and clarity. Online access to just about every image available makes it *easier* to find the picture, piece of art, or graphic; teachers who know how to use visuals effectively can make them an integral, meaningful part of their lessons.

Let's take a look, then, at some visual and technological support systems that can assist teachers with the interactive classroom.

Seek Clarity and Simplicity

Photos, graphs, charts, and maps not only add visual impact to a presentation that might otherwise be totally auditory but are necessary additions for those whose dominant learning style is visual. Incorporating visuals into instruction has other benefits as well. Something as simple as posting visual directions that can be easily seen as students enter the room can be powerful. Whatever the medium for this (blackboard or whiteboard, chart, overhead transparency), it probably helps to display it in the same manner and in the same location each day so students will know where to look.

In the 1950s, when I was growing up in Pennsylvania, black and white was the rule in photos and on television. Color was the exception. The reverse is true today; color is the norm and black-and-white images are rare, *something that can be used to a teacher's advantage.* Advertisers today will often use black-and-white imagery or a single (spot) color in both print and TV advertising precisely because it is novel and catches the viewer's attention. One of the most successful Super Bowl commercials of all time (the 1984 introduction of the MacIntosh Computer by Apple) used contrasting color and black and white imagery to incredible effect. That commercial is still stunning 35 years after its debut. It was completely novel, and anything that qualifies as a novelty is particularly useful for that very reason. In fact, novelty "creates a stronger opportunity for new learning and pathways in the brain" (Jensen, 2005a, p. 120).

As demonstrated earlier in this chapter, a piece of white chart paper and a black marker can be particularly effective as a visual communication tool in classrooms, again because of the *stark contrast* between that simple medium and the steady diet of swiftly transitioning color images to which we have become accustomed. Garmston and Wellman (1992) suggest using charts "when you have big ideas that you want to keep present in the room for reference. These also become anchors

Tactical Tip

To provide a bit of novelty in your classroom, locate a chart stand, a pad of chart paper, and a box of water-based markers of different colors. Remove the yellow, pink, and light blue markers (too hard to see at a distance). When you want a list made, find a student with some pretty good printing skills, and have her stand to the side of the chart stand with two different dark-colored markers. (I use combinations of orange and brown, blue and red, or black and any other darkish color.) While you facilitate a brainstorming session, ask the student with the markers to use alternating colors in the creation of the list. Make sure you pause long enough when given a piece of information to allow her to finish or almost finish the entry. The use of alternating colors allows people looking at the chart to distinguish easily between one entry and another. The use of the chart itself, rather than a whiteboard or overhead transparency, provides novelty, something the brain craves.

for future sessions with this audience" (p. 69). Of course, an electronic whiteboard can be used for the same thing, but in a building full of that technology, white charts and a few markers of different colors may provide the visual variety needed to make an impact.

Measure Twice, Cut Once

There is an age-old adage for carpenters—measure twice, cut once. Accuracy is necessary when constructing fine furniture or renovating the kitchen. The same is true for adult or student presenters as they prepare visuals for a presentation. Teams getting ready to present in the not-too-distant future would do well to rehearse everything a few times, and that includes the use of graphs or charts projected on screens for the audience. Visuals should be accurate, highly visible, easy to understand, and grammatically correct. I have seen a single spelling error cause an audience to discount the message. Check the math, the spelling, the grammar, the size and positioning of graphic elements, and the font size of any headline or copy. Measure twice, cut once.

A few suggestions for teachers and students when it comes to the use of charts as visual supports for presentations:

1. Make sure everything placed on the chart is visible from all corners of the room. When setting up to present at a conference or in a school gym or cafeteria, I display several slides from my presentation on the screen while moving around the room. I can check the focus and see if the smallest point size I have used in a piece of copy is visible from everywhere in the room. If it is too small, I increase it. Take the seat of several members of your audience, and make sure you can see clearly what you want your audience to see.

2. For teachers and students using PowerPoint or a similar presentation system, make sure you use a remote, and take the image to a black screen when you are done referring to it. Visuals become your competitors if you are talking while an image is displayed. Again, if you are referring to it as you speak, leave it there. Otherwise, go to black screen until you are ready to move on. Remember, visuals are powerful, and you will not be able to compete with something on the screen. Use what is on the screen, but don't try to compete with it.

3. Finally, students are sometimes tempted to use graphics that wiggle, bounce, fly, or shake. The problem with these images is that they are distracting. I once watched as a basketball bounced up and down for the entire time a presenter was speaking about the information on that slide. I looked around, noticing that others were fixated on the bouncing ball, too. My guess is that few members of her audience heard anything she said. She had created her own competition, and she was losing the game. Images that fall into the "cutsie" category are by their very nature highly distracting. Keep it clear and keep it simple.

Here are some questions related to visuals students can wrestle with in standing pairs:

- In what ways do visuals support presentations?
- Can visuals like graphs, charts, or other graphics be too complex? If so, how?

- What kinds of visuals might distract from your presentation?
- Why is it important to rehearse every aspect of your presentation in front of someone other than your own project teammates?

Provide Process Time

Teachers who have just covered some new information on the overhead should give students a chance to process the material and ask questions (Allen, 2008, p. 95). In fact, if they have been sitting for a few minutes, have them stand up, pair up, and discuss the material. If it helps to have a relevant image on the screen, then leave the projector on. If not, turn it off while they share. If the lights were dimmed, bring them back up for the discussion. This opportunity for student processing is what may be missing from many classroom lessons that use overhead projectors, slide presentations, or any other electronic visual image.

While observing in an elementary classroom, I watched as the teacher displayed an image of the famous aviator, Amelia Earhart, on the screen. Wrapped around the image were a couple of biographical paragraphs on Earhart; most of the students and I were drawn to the photograph and to the copy. I have no doubt that many of her students, having first taken in the picture, had begun to read the paragraphs. The teacher interrupted our reverie, however, and began to read the paragraph out loud. This caused a great deal of dissonance on my part and, I suspect, on the part of many of her students. We could stop reading and try to listen, we could try to continue reading and tune her out, or we could simply opt out of the whole exercise altogether.

The lesson here is this: Presenters who display an image of any kind should provide time for participants to look at it, give some thought to its meaning, and otherwise deal with it individually. If it is likely participants will read the copy on their own, it is best to let them read it while you read it silently to yourself. Look around when you are done reading; if they are done, go to black on the screen and lead whatever conversation in which you want them to participate, in pairs or as a whole-class discussion. Overwhelming students with a visual image while the teacher talks about it is likely to lead to confusion and, unfortunately, disengagement on the part of those the whole exercise is meant to benefit.

Verbal Miscues

If active listening and eye contact are critical skills, the proper use of voice is something that needs to be considered by teachers in their role as presenters. My guess is that every teacher can remember a presenter who spoke in a monotone or laced his or her monologue with *verbalized pauses*, like "um" or "you know." Speaking in a monotone quickly hypnotizes students, and verbalized pauses serve to distract them to the point where they can even begin to count the number of times the teacher says "um." Trying to multitask like this will cause the level of retention and understanding to be held to a minimum on the part of listeners; the good news is that such problems can be avoided.

> *Speaking in a monotone quickly hypnotizes students, and verbalized pauses serve to distract them to the point where they can even begin to count the number of times the teacher says "um."*

On more than one occasion in the early 1990s, I had myself videotaped presenting to student and adult audiences. The tape revealed several things of which I had been unaware. First, I used verbal pauses ("um" was my favorite) with mind-numbing regularity. Second, I had a tendency to use too many hand and arm gestures, another distraction for those in the audience. Finally, I found that my voice tended to drop off at the end of many of my sentences. Over the years, I have been able to correct most of these deficiencies, *but it was those videotapes that uncovered them for me*. I really had no idea I was doing those things. These problems with my presentation style had been, I am certain, obvious to my students and adult audiences, *but not to me*. The bad news is that the tape doesn't lie. The *good* news is that the tape doesn't lie.

Video of teachers in action can reveal a great deal about what they are or are not doing. Fisher and Frey (2019) call the practice of recording a short clip of a teacher in action, then taking the time to discuss it with the teacher, microteaching. The problem with normal debriefs after a coach, colleague, or administrator observes a class is that the feedback can be pretty one-sided. Some teachers become resistant to such feedback "because they have a pre-existing 'confirmation bias' about their teaching and only accept examples that confirm what they already believe" (pp. 82–83). Even a short video clip capturing the teacher's actions and the students' reactions can make for an interesting—and highly useful—discussion related not just to teaching but to learning, affirm Fisher and Frey.

The Mighty Pause

In a career that has included teaching, training, and educational sales, I have come to agree with Grinder (2000) that "the pause is the single most powerful non-verbal signal that can be used" (p. 62). One of its most effective uses is as a replacement for verbalized pauses like "um" or "you know." A *short pause* allows the teacher to think or refocus, does the same for the students, and is not in itself a distraction.

Great comedians are master presenters, and the best of them understand the power of the pause. Jack Benny, in radio and on television, cultivated the persona of a penny-pincher. In one comedy sequence, Benny is held at gunpoint by a robber who demands of Benny, "Your money or your life!" After what seems an interminable moment of silence, the robber prompts Benny once again: "I said, your money or your life!" At which point Benny replies, "I'm thinking! I'm thinking!" The audience does not wait for the response to begin laughing. I have seen this routine countless times, and what amazes me is how long Benny draws out that pause. His eventual response is almost anticlimactic. It represents the masterful use of a nonverbal.

Silence can also be used to help the audience (and the presenter) refocus. My own experience as a teacher and my observations of other teachers over the years has convinced me that we sometimes talk almost incessantly *because we are not comfortable with silence*. This is why providing wait time is difficult for teachers. It also explains why, when I began using *think-write-pair-share* as an instructional strategy, I had a problem with providing enough time for the thinking phase. The silence was as deafening as it was disconcerting for me. For periods of extended silence to be effective, the teacher is not the only person in the room who needs to feel comfortable with it. A critical stage in the formation of a class comes when students, too, feel right at home with silence (Grinder, 2000).

Getting students to participate is sometimes as simple as pausing at the end of a sentence and letting them supply the last word or phrase. The teacher has to be fairly certain, of course, that the students can successfully fill in the blank.

Tactical Tip

There is a natural tendency for teachers wanting to emphasize something as particularly important to raise their voices at the end of a sentence. A student who inhabits many classrooms during the day will hear this tactic used over and over, until it becomes invisible and ineffective. Try this: When you are making an important point and want to verbally underline the last few words, try pausing for a beat, then lowering the volume of your voice. Deliver those words confidently—*and softly*. I have seen this used to great effect by professional presenters and teachers alike. It is not what students expect; *therefore, it has impact.*

For example, to drive a point home, a teacher may say, "Which just goes to show you that what goes around _____." Near the end of the sentence, the teacher cups one ear with a hand and turns it toward the students, inviting them to complete the thought. It is novel, often funny, and it does, I have found, underline whatever concept I am trying to highlight. John Almarode, who wrote the foreword to this book, uses this strategy to perfection in his college classrooms and in his presentations.

What follows are several presentation-related questions students can deal with in standing pairs:

- Why is providing time for audience members to process information so important?

- What could you and a team preparing to present your project findings learn from taking a look at a video of a presentation rehearsal?

- What ways of getting your attention have some of your teachers used? If one or two are particularly effective, why do you think that is?

- How does pausing during a presentation help the presenter? The audience?

Humor

Virtually all the great teachers and presenters I have seen and known over the years have incorporated (appropriate) humor into their presentation skill sets. Most of these successful and effective educators have had as a powerful tool a self-deprecating humor that served as a good model for their students and audience participants. In classrooms where healthy laughter is abundant, the environment is positive and learning is actually facilitated (Tate, 2003). Humor also has positive physiological effects. Costa (2000) counts among humor's positive effects "a drop in the pulse rate, secretion of endorphins, and increased oxygen in the blood" (p. 36). Humor is a powerful door opener into the day's lesson and into the content, and teachers can work to make laughter an integral part of the classroom routine.

> Humor is a powerful door opener into the day's lesson and into the content, and teachers can work to make laughter an integral part of the classroom routine.

Some teachers are naturally funny and don't seem to have to work at it. For those among us who want to interject humor into our role as presenters in the classroom, here are some ways to do that appropriately.

1. Jensen (2000a) suggests asking students to stand (always energizing) and "practice a big group laugh" (p. 44).

2. Teachers will often come across humorous stories or anecdotes that can be shared with students. Earlier, I mentioned the use of a captain's chair or stool somewhere in the classroom as the location for telling stories. This special seat could be used for any number of humorous stories, appropriate jokes, or anecdotes. In fact, students could use the stool as well, having been invited by the teacher to share a humorous story or joke from that location.

3. When teachers are willing to make fun of their own mistakes, but never of anyone else's, they signal that making fun of someone else is not appropriate behavior. There have been occasions when *my mistakes* have formed the basis for a running gag throughout a class period or even extending over several days.

4. Done (2006) says that he constantly does things to get his students to laugh, and many of those things include using different voices, using cartoons, standing on his chair, and laughing at himself over incidents the students are bound to find funny. "I always tell my students about the time I got my tie caught in the laminator. I thought I was going to die!" (p. 35).

5. Every teacher has been in a situation where an extended period of laughter tends to keep everyone from getting back to business quickly. After establishing that laughter is perfectly acceptable in the classroom, suggests Smith (2004), the teacher can teach the students a "postlaugh" signal that communicates that it is time to get back to work (p. 94). I can remember a teacher who would purposely build the laughter to a crescendo by raising his hands palms up until the noise was just this side of deafening and then cut it all off by dropping his hands in much the same way as a band director making sure all the musicians stopped at the same moment.

The use of appropriate humor assists in "building a climate of connectedness and safety" (Bluestein, 2001, p. 215). Sarcasm is one example of inappropriate humor. Sarcastic "remarks directed to students that demean, tease, or deride, can, at minimum, hinder or incapacitate higher level thinking" (Jensen, 1995, as cited in Tate, 2003, p. 37). Sarcasm in a classroom where the teacher is trying to move students from a passive to an active mode is counterproductive. Teachers need to model the appropriate use of humor and indicate what *will not* be tolerated.

Figure 5.1   Fishbone Diagram

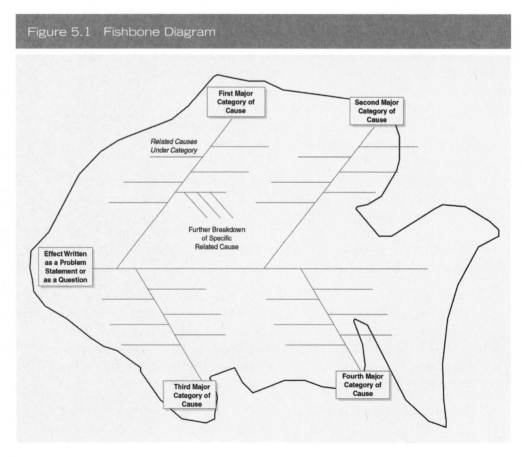

Source: Dianne Kinnison.

Figure 5.2 Flow Chart

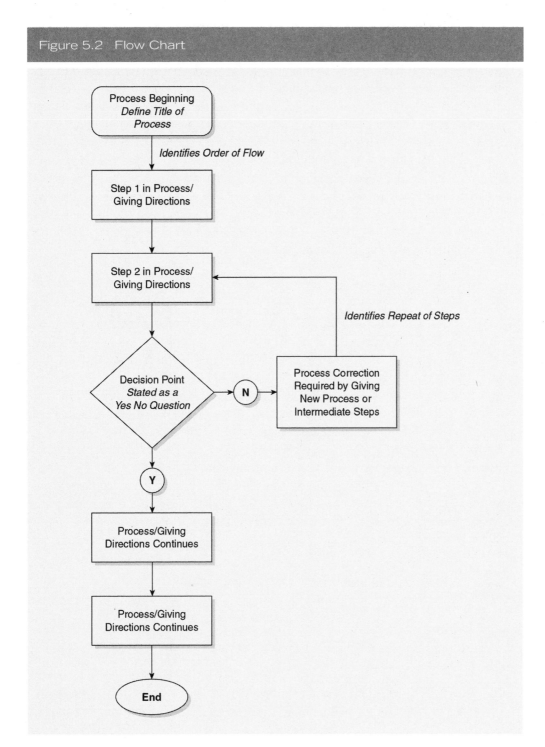

Source: Dianne Kinnison.

Graphic Organizers

Parry and Gregory (1998) identify graphic organizers as "metacognitive tools in a visual form" that "allow students to organize data into manageable and comprehensible chunks" (p. 168). Teachers should not, according to Wicks, Peregoy, and Wheeler (2001), see powerful tools such as fishbone diagrams and flowcharts as add-ons but as tools that "will help [them] tackle the curriculum—more efficiently and more effectively" (p. 167). Fishbone diagrams (Figure 5.1) help students with cause and effect and can be used in almost any subject area. Flowcharts (Figure 10.3) assist students in visualizing sequence. Students who are high visual are particularly well served by graphic organizers, but my experience has been that students in general appreciate the efficacy of these visual tools.

Some of my colleagues and I watched one morning as a third-grade student led a discussion of a story everyone had read. She used a fishbone to great effect as she explored cause and effect for something that happened in the story. She asked questions of her peers, and she did a wonderful job of facilitating a whole-class discussion. A fishbone like the one above served as the centerpiece of the conversation. Her teacher told us later that her students were used to using graphic organizers and leading their peers in substantive conversations. It was quite remarkable the way her students had honed their presentation and group facilitation skills.

YOUR TURN

Someone once said if you're not modeling what you're teaching, you're teaching something else. In a highly competitive workplace environment where communication and collaboration are more important than ever, teachers need to model excellent presentation skills on a daily basis. Teachers who are confident and highly competent presenters give students a high standard they can emulate as they develop their own skill sets along these lines. The Common Core State Standards highlight the development of excellent speaking skills, and teachers who consistently model those skills will facilitate the continuous improvement process of students trying to improve their oral communication abilities.

In an age where project-based learning is in more and more districts and schools, student presentations are becoming more frequent. Presenting alone is one thing, but working as a team is something else entirely. Presentation teams can capitalize on the strengths of various members of the team. Teachers can help by providing modeling, as we have seen, and by making sure feedback mechanisms are in place to support continuous improvement.

REFLECTIVE QUESTIONS

Is there someone in the building or district who can spend some time digitally recording presentations or your own classes? (The librarian in one of the middle schools in which I taught taped two of my classes for me, and it was extremely helpful. This involves risk because it is disconcerting to see oneself on the screen, but it provides valuable feedback.)

The next time you are in a conference session or a workshop or faculty meeting, take notice of the size of the type on the screen during a slide presentation. Can you read it from where you are? (If not, make a mental note not to do this in the classroom or in a presentation to adults. Point sizes of 24 or larger are best in a classroom setting.)

If students are expected to present to peers or adults, how can you develop low-risk practice sessions for the teams?

How could you best model the use of appropriate humor, a fishbone diagram, purposeful movement, the mighty pause, the proper use of visuals, and other presentation skills listed in this chapter?

In what ways can you see to it that plenty of feedback is forthcoming for practice sessions for students working on presentations related to project-based learning or for any presentations they may be required to make? (Could students develop presentation rubrics they can use regularly?)

CHAPTER 6

Let's Be Clear

There I was one early December morning, facilitating a workshop in Williamsburg, Virginia, with about 70 teachers and administrators as participants. They were standing in pairs, and each participant held a laminated card. I announced that when I gave the signal, they should talk with their respective partners about what their cards had in common, then trade cards and find a new partner, continuing the conversations with different participants until I told them to stop. Feeling, no doubt, that my instructions were clear and eminently understandable, I was about to set the activity in motion when an administrator close to me leaned in and whispered, "Our cards are laminated, rectangular, and blue!"

He had, of course, seized upon a weak point in my directions; I wanted participants to compare the *text* on the cards, not the size, color, or shape, *but I hadn't said that*. I wasn't clear about what I wanted them to do. I buried my face in my hands, called a time out, shared with everyone what he had told me, and did what I should have done in the first place: *I modeled what they were supposed to do*.

That helpful administrator had reacted the way any elementary, middle, or high school student might have done under the same circumstances—by interpreting what they thought I wanted them to do in a way I had not intended yet in a way that made perfect sense given my (ambiguous) instructions. In a classroom setting, it could have played out much longer, and I might have had to stop everything midactivity and bring everyone back to square one for the new set of directions, something guaranteed to cause confusion and bring any forward momentum to a standstill.

Veteran teachers may recall occasions where students followed directions that may not have been entirely clear, at which point it became necessary to bring everything to a screeching halt and start over again. For teachers, working the room after turning students loose on an in-class project or assignment is made much more difficult when hand after hand goes up from those unsure about how to proceed. Teachers who want to be able to concentrate on content-related issues should ensure that instructions are clearly understood by students. One of the most effective ways I know to clarify in the minds of students what we want them to do involves the kind of modeling I *should* have done in Williamsburg on that December day.

> *Teachers who want to be able to concentrate on content-related issues should ensure that instructions are clearly understood by students.*

Do as I Do

On that occasion, I got lazy and subsequently left the ambiguity door wide open. All I had to do to remedy this was employ a quick and effective bit of modeling: I brought one of the participants to act as my temporary partner, then held one of the blue cards (text-side out) at eye level so my partner could read it, while he did the same. It took only a second or two, but it clarified everything relating to exactly what I wanted compared during the paired conversations. If the process is not clear, the content will be lost in the inevitable confusion that follows.

I am often in classrooms with more than one adult (another teacher, a teacher assistant or paraprofessional, or a parent volunteer), and this means the person facilitating the process can arrange in advance to have someone with whom to pair when it comes to modeling. I worked with several elementary teachers as we had their students practice the structured conversation activity called paired verbal fluency (PVF; Chapter 4). This provided students with an opportunity to practice their oral language skills (eye contact, body language, summarization, asking for clarification, etc.), and throughout the 2 days I was in the building, each classroom teacher and I modeled an entire PVF activity using the same topic we were asking them to use in their own discussions. Because we took turns in speaking and listening mode, the students in each classroom had two opportunities to observe what it was we wanted them to do.

High Operational Standards

I once watched a middle school student try to write in a journal that was perched on a book bag; the ultimate result of this was as predictable as it was inevitable. It wasn't long before the book bag and the journal fell off the side of the desk and onto the floor to the merriment of the rest of the students and to the chagrin of the teacher. I have seen classrooms where teachers distribute large sheets of chart paper only to have students discover there is no room on the quad (four desks pushed together) for the chart paper and the other relevant materials. In some classrooms, students try in vain to locate materials they will need in the next 15 minutes. The resultant confusion and periods of chaos make working the room more difficult for teachers, and it is unnecessary.

In each of these cases, not enough work went into pretask planning; teachers in presentation mode must facilitate process in ways that guarantee students are operating in work environments conducive to the task at hand. There is no reason for book bags, purses, or any other extraneous items to be on work surfaces that need to be ready for an activity or project. Teachers who assume students will *automatically* think through what needs to be moved or supplied for a given task may subsequently spend a good deal of time troubleshooting process-related problems at a time when they would prefer working on *content* with students.

Too often teachers give *auditory* instructions when it comes to how student work areas should look, including what materials they need for the next task. Because students have learned to filter out teacher talk, verbal directions may not get through. The fourth grader who needs his journal and pencil in the next 30 seconds did not process this simple set of instructions. In another classroom, that group of eighth graders giggling in the back corner of the room just missed a set of verbal directions instructing them to clean off their quad and pick up a large sheet of chart paper and several markers for the next activity. The problem

Because students have learned to filter out teacher talk, verbal directions may not get through.

here is one of clarity and operational efficiency. Students are not clear as to what materials are necessary. What needed to be accomplished in preparation for a specific task was transmitted verbally but not received.

Teachers constantly give directions to their students, and in an elementary classroom, this happens on scores of occasions during the course of a single day. When desks and work areas are not ready to go for the next activity or assignment, teachers often blame students for not "paying attention," and I have seen this—and *done* this—more times than I can remember. Because students miss the auditory cues and instructions, teachers get frustrated and *want* to say—and on occasion *do* say—things like, "Am I not being clear?" or, "What part of needing a journal and a pencil did you not understand?" or, "Am I talking to *myself* here?" or, with head buried in hands, "I could have gone into real estate!" Working the room every day is difficult enough without talking to oneself.

As Medina (2008) notes, "Vision trumps all other senses." Anyone who has watched a teenager on an airplane play a single video game hour after hour would no doubt agree with Medina when he writes, "Vision is by far our most dominant sense, taking up half our brain's resources" (p. 240). Therefore, when we give only auditory directions (and all at once), we are not playing to our students' strengths. In a world where students watch hours of video images on screens of every size and description, relying solely on auditory directions is almost always going to be problematic. My sense is every veteran teacher has experienced this, but there is a way out. There is a solution, and I did not discover it until a few years ago. There is something that will help teachers communicate exactly how student desks should look at a given time and for a stated purpose, with no ambiguity whatsoever.

> In a world where students watch hours of video images on screens of every size and description, relying solely on auditory directions is almost always going to be problematic.

I recommend teachers go visual with directions related to how desk and work areas should be set up, and what I'm going to suggest is quite inexpensive. In the age of digital photography, it costs nothing at all as long as a teacher can put his or her hands on a digital camera or a cell phone that provides a high-resolution image. Figure 6.1 shows a desk with exactly what the teacher wants students to have for the next activity—a journal and a pencil. There can be no question as to what should be on the students' desks before moving to the task at hand. No book bags, no textbooks, no purses, no cell phones—just a journal and a pencil. Some teachers will play a particular piece of upbeat music that triggers the 30-second period necessary to get everything else off the desks, even as the journal and the pencil are placed on desks, ready to go. Again, the image leaves no room for ambiguity; every student knows what needs to be done.

Figure 6.2 shows a quad setup with a piece of chart paper and the accompanying materials needed for the forthcoming activity. There are teachers at all levels who have a single desktop file full of such photos, ready for use at the click of a mouse. Once one of these images is projected onto the screen, there is nothing the teacher has to say. *There is no auditory component and no resultant confusion.* This procedure can be practiced until students have the process down. As new classroom transitions and work area setups become necessary, the teacher adds a new photo to the file. Again, working the room becomes far easier and less frustrating when going visual can provide clarity.

I once met a science teacher whose students worked in lab settings often using a great deal of equipment. Students would get to their stations without what they needed, and she spent a good deal of time troubleshooting *process*—time she would rather have spent dealing with *content*. She located a digital camera, stood on a stool looking down at her lab stations, and shot picture after picture of exactly how she wanted the stations

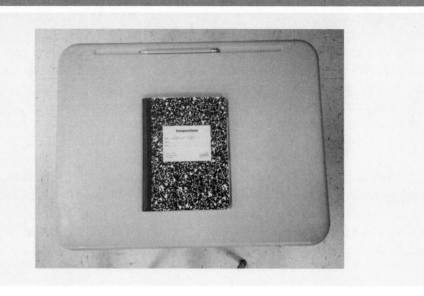

Figure 6.1   This image provides clarity as to what is expected for the next activity.

Source: Photo by Kathy Galford.

Figure 6.2   This visual clarifies how the quads should look.

Source: Photo by Kathy Galford.

to look for various activities. She would display the appropriate image on the screen in the front of the room, give her science students a time limit, and wait. If auditory setup instructions are problematic, *then shift to visual.*

Some student desks at the elementary school level have an enclosed shelf, or "cubby," underneath the top of the desk, providing storage space for necessary materials. In many middle and high schools, classrooms may have the welded desk/chair units like that shown in Figure 6.3. In this sixth-grade classroom, students kept scissors, glue sticks,

68   The InterActive Classroom

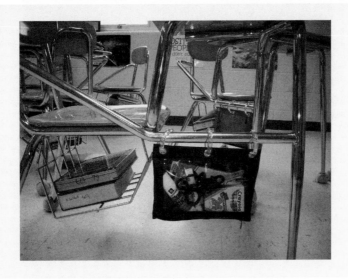

Source: Photo by Kathy Galford.

markers, and much else in transparent bags attached to one of the cross bars. Having materials at the ready saves time that might otherwise be spent rooting through boxes or large containers for things needed for an activity or project.

One at a Time

Apparently, intelligence services all over the world have the ability to send out instructions to agents in short communication bursts that can later be decoded, understood, and subsequently acted on. Students who are the recipients of short bursts of directions from their teachers don't have access to any sophisticated electronic devices that would allow them to slow everything down and sort it all out after transmission. Teachers who fully understand what they want done often give several directions at once—and suffer the consequences, along with their students:

> Mrs. Martin rattles off a five-step set of directions and says, "Go!" Connie hears Steps 1 and 2 but is distracted and misses Steps 3, 4, and 5. Justin tunes in for 3, 4, and 5 but misses 1 and 2 and is now searching right and left for help. Eddie is—as Eddie always is—in a better place in his mind from the beginning and misses the whole sequence; he is now madly waving his hand in the air, adding to the annoyance of a teacher who can't figure out why she got all the slow kids.

The problem here, of course, is that the teacher knows *exactly* what she wants done, but her short burst of instructions was lost in the translation.

Had she given those directions one at a time, she and her students would have avoided all the pain and suffering that comes with too many directions given too quickly. If the activity requires a set of markers, then let them get the markers first, followed by—one at a time—whatever else is necessary. A visual might be helpful here, but if not, then give the directions one step at a time until the point where what is necessary *intersects with what needs to be accomplished.* If too much too fast is confusing, then slow it down.

Let's imagine a middle school teacher wants her students to follow the viewing of a short video selection with a standing pair share, where students discuss the video with their notes or learning logs in hand. There is no need to take students all the way through what they are going to do up front.

My recommendation is to have students identify their learning partners (Step 1); wave at their partners (Step 2); pick up their notes, along with a pencil (Step 3); move with their materials to the accompaniment of some upbeat music until each student is paired with his or her learning partner (Step 4); and then turn and face the teacher (Step 5). These essential process-related steps can be accomplished quickly, and it makes working the room simple for the classroom teacher. Once students are facing the teacher, she can give them the *final* set of instructions—in this case, to discuss their notes with a partner while answering the two questions on the board in the process.

The idea here is to get from Step 1 to Step 5 without process-related difficulties. All the teacher has to do is take her students through the steps one at a time while checking to make sure everyone has done what needs to be done along the way. The alternative is to give the information in those short bursts, only to have students forget what they need to do. Working the room becomes much easier if this step-by-step system is employed whenever multiple process-related directions are necessary. I have found that students appreciate this kind of efficiency; most students don't like confusion when it comes to what needs to get done in the classroom.

Tactical Tip

Here is an example of a set of clear directions, given one at a time in order to avoid confusion:

- *Verbal cue 1:* "Look this way, please." (Wait until you have eye contact around the room.)

- *Verbal cue 2:* "Check the appointment clock on the inside cover of your log to see who your 12:00 partner is." (wait)

- *Verbal cue 3:* "Wave at your partner." (If someone's 12:00 partner is absent, now is the time to deal with it.)

- *Verbal cue 4:* "Stand behind your desk." (If you want empty hands when they move into standing pairs, this is your opportunity to make sure all hands are free.)

Remove Barriers to the Message

As a young teacher more than four decades ago, I spent a good deal of time in the faculty lounge complaining about a lack of time and the abundance of material to be covered. Teachers can't change the fact that the amount of classroom time available with students is limited, but I would make the argument that we can adjust the *how* of what we do in ways that maximize the use of precious minutes by learning to work the room efficiently. The truth is that teachers often put hurdles in their own way, self-inflicted barriers that slow everything down and inhibit the learning process.

As an example, imagine a classroom where the teacher projects an image on the screen and then begins to talk to his students while they are still trying to come to grips with the image. Picture a classroom where the teacher projects a couple of paragraphs onto the electronic whiteboard and then begins to read that text to her students even as many of them are trying to read it for themselves. We hear about multitasking, and one might think that students are fully capable of reading the copy on the screen while listening to the teacher.

It doesn't happen that way because the brain *does not work that way*. Students can listen to the teacher or read the text. They can ponder the picture on the screen, or they can listen to the teacher tell them what it is they are seeing. They can read the copy, or they can listen to the teacher read the copy. They can come to grips with the image, or they can listen to the teacher; they can't do both.

Teachers who unveil a beautiful photo or interesting graphic on the screen need to give students time to take it all in. Let them register and process what they are seeing. Beyond this, I suggest teachers who have projected an image on the screen have students stand, pair, and discuss with partners what they see. Once students have had a chance to see it, discuss it, and perhaps ask some questions, *they are invested in it*.

- Step 1 is to project the image.

- Step 2 is to let them think about and talk about what they see.

- Step 3 is to ask them to raise a few questions with a partner, questions they can subsequently ask of the teacher.

This is the doorway to the information; too many teachers project something on the screen, *only to spend a few minutes explaining it*. My experience is that when teachers do this, students gradually begin to go to a better place in their minds.

When teachers do all the explaining when it comes to what students are seeing or when they read out loud what *students* could read on their own, this short-circuits the learning process. If a photo or graphic is important, let students have some time to ponder it and make whatever connections they can make with their own experience and the content. If a couple of paragraphs are on the screen, let students read them on their own. There is time for whatever else teachers want to do later on, but don't put barriers in the way of their thought processes. Let *them* read; let *them* contemplate; let *them* talk about what they read and what they see. We need to provide enough time so that students can *reflect* on new information, independently or with a partner. When time is limited, we need to turn more of it over to students.

- *Verbal cue 5:* "Stand with your 12:00 partner somewhere in the room."

- *Verbal cue 6:* "Look this way, please." (Now you can give them their instructions as to what they will be doing as standing pair share partners. The time may come when you can begin with cue 5, but if confusion ensues, return to the multicue approach. The goal is to have them in standing pairs, facing you.)

Tactical Tip

Many teachers and presenters, including me, use PowerPoint or some other presentation program to display images on the screen. I suggest you have your remote close at hand, giving you the ability to quickly darken the screen. When you don't need the image, *get rid of it*. A visual like that competes with you for attention. Students may fixate on a picture, a bit of graphic detail, a vibrant color, or a piece of copy. *This means they are not listening.* You are talking, but they are concentrating on the image(s). When you are ready to highlight something visually, one click on the remote gives you the slide which you (now) want them to see and on which you want them to reflect. (And change the batteries in your remote frequently. I once watched as a teacher clicked again and again, only to realize the batteries had finally given up the ghost.)

We need to provide enough time so that students can reflect on new information, independently or with a partner.

Clear and Unambiguous Feedback

Good feedback provides clarity. Bad feedback invites confusion and ambiguity. Generally, perhaps, we think of feedback as it applies to improving student work, and this is certainly half of it. The other half has to do with how it informs instruction. No coach can

Tactical Tip

When students work alone or in groups, the teacher's place is out and about, not sequestered behind his desk. There is much you can learn by circulating while students work. You can observe, ask questions, encourage, coach—and build rapport. The feedback teachers provide while making the rounds is important; when teachers ignore what students are doing, this amounts to negative feedback for *them*. It says what they are doing is less important than what the teacher is doing at his desk. A fifth-grade teacher I observed used to hunker down next to his students as they worked, and his kids grew to count on what he called quality time.

Without feedback, neither students nor teachers can know what adjustments to make on the journey to improved performance and instruction.

begin to improve the performance of his or her team without feedback. Coaches learn from what they see and hear in practice and during the games, they learn from what their players say and do, and they learn from team films and from assistant coaches. To coaches, teachers, principals, and superintendents, feedback is the lifeblood of continuous improvement. Feedback accelerates progress on the part of players and students, and it informs instruction for coaches, teachers, and administrators.

When a teacher writes "Great job!" on a term paper, and if there is nothing to explain what that means, it doesn't really help a student who wants to know what needs to be improved—or why. Eddie may feel good temporarily reading that complimentary phrase; he may also infer that "Great job!" means there is absolutely nothing in his effort that needs adjusting or improving. I would prefer to see teachers give fewer assignments and make certain these assignments receive sufficient and effective feedback—from teachers and peers.

While working on an in-class writing assignment, Eddie must know he can rely on his classmates and his teacher to let him know how he is doing. This is valuable for Eddie *and* his teacher. As long as we must assign grades, we will have summative assessments, but students need constant, formative checkpoints along the way. "Teachers need to know on a daily basis what is working for each of their students and what is not," affirm Conzemius and O'Neill (2006), "and then use that information to support or to change current instructional practices" (p. 58). Without feedback, neither students nor teachers can know what adjustments to make on the journey to improved performance and instruction.

Teachers may spend a great deal of time providing feedback for individual students, and this is necessary, to be sure. In photographic terms, this is equivalent to microphotography, and teachers can spend hours working hard to improve student performance. Once teachers take this microlevel look at how their students are doing individually, they need to zoom out and take a macrolevel approach to the feedback they provided. Taken in its entirety, the feedback provided for an entire class set of papers may say much about what—and how well—something is taught. Dougherty (2012) analyzed sets of class papers, concluding "that a task—sometimes an assignment, sometimes not—accompanied by a class set of papers tells a lot about the effectiveness of instruction because a class set reveals what was taught and wasn't taught in the classroom" (p. 17). If feedback is to inform instruction, teachers must be willing, individually or in collaboration with colleagues on continuous-improvement teams, to take a wider view of assessment results—formative or summative.

One way in which teachers can provide valuable—and personal—feedback is through teacher–student conferences. I am in classrooms constantly, observing teachers observe students, and I can say from long experience that when a teacher takes the time to hunker down next to a student and deliver meaningful feedback, students appreciate it. Davis, Summers, and Miller (2012) report a "consistent finding from the field of educational psychology is that our messages, or verbal feedback, to students significantly affects how they feel about themselves and their schoolwork" (p. 89). When I observe planned or impromptu teacher–student conferences, I watch the students when the teacher walks away, and more often than not, their body language communicates satisfaction and appreciation.

"Why are we doing this?"

I'm guessing most teachers have, at one time or another, heard this age-old query on the part of a student. Questions like this, affirm Almarode and Vandas (2018), serve as "a clear sign that something is amiss with the learning intention. Students not only want clarity about what they are to learn, but they require this clarification for any goal-oriented behavior to be attempted or accomplished" (p. 30). The authors provide a math-related learning intention that makes it clear what is expected: *I can explain how graphing ordered pairs helps me to predict and compare data.*

Teaching is hard enough without adding confusion to what the learning intentions are. It is possible students will work on a project for some time before realizing exactly what the goal is. "Good learning intentions," writes Hattie (2012), "are those that make clear to the students the type or level of performance that they need to attain, so that they understand where and when to invest energies, strategies, and thinking, and where they are positioned along the trajectory towards successful learning" (p. 52). Students need to understand what is expected of them, and feedback mechanisms will help students understand where they are on the way to where they need to be.

"Who is making the decision here?"

I have also found there is a great deal of collective satisfaction that comes from successful outcomes planned and executed by colleagues working in teams. Brainstorming, researching, hashing and rehashing possible ways forward, figuring out implementation guidelines and timelines; all this can be exhausting work that is worth it if what has been decided gets done. But I have also seen teams work for days, weeks, or months on a project, only to be disappointed in the end *because they were unclear as to what their role was in the decision-making process.* There is little more frustrating for a team than learning that their role was simply to suggest possible solutions to a problem, when the general understanding was that they were responsible for the final decision.

Teachers or administrators asked to work on an improvement team should attempt to find out up front, before work begins, who the decision maker is and what role the team has in the process. Otherwise, team members may not be willing to invest time and effort in the project. Garmston and von Frank (2012) provide a warning for school teams about to embark on important collaborative efforts:

> The effect of not knowing who will make the final decision and what processes will be used can create broken trust. And when members lose trust in the process, groups may become embroiled in

> ### Tactical Tip
>
> When asked to work on an improvement team at the building or district level, don't be afraid to inquire as to who is making the final decision after the work of the team is done. Your time is valuable, and clarity when it comes to your role and the role of your prospective team is essential. If yours is an advisory role, fine, but get that clear up front. If your team will give a series of recommendations, one of which will serve as the way forward, great, but again, find that out before you agree to immerse yourself in this important work. Decisions are made at lots of levels, and that is fine. *To those working on the team, it is a matter of clarity.*

second-guessing, may become resistant, or may experience lengthy and unproductive process arguments. This robs them of time; more importantly, it saps group energy, diminishes members' sense of efficacy, and lessens their motivation to persevere on important topics. (p. 37)

If the final decision on anything related to school improvement rests in the hands of the building administrative team and if the role of the improvement team is one of recommending possible ways forward, then they should know that. Moreover, members of the team should not be shy about seeking clarification as to the totality of the decision-making process. If a team knows in advance that theirs is an advisory role, so be it. They can function happily with the full understanding that they are not being tasked with the final decision. I have experienced firsthand the disappointment and frustration that comes when a team finds out late in the game that they misunderstood their role in the whole process, and I have seen the positive and long-lasting results when team members were clear about their role.

Teachers appreciate being asked for input and feedback when changes are in the wind, but nothing beats being an integral part of the decision-making process. "When truly empowered to make decisions, solve problems, and construct viable and potentially powerful planning that will benefit students and staff members alike, teachers appreciate the opportunity to become genuinely engaged in meaningful continuous-improvement dialogue" (Nash & Hwang, 2013, pp. 21–22). Everyone in the school community benefits from effective school improvement efforts, and teachers take a great deal of satisfaction from being part of such efforts.

The staff and students of Great Bridge Primary School in Virginia moved into a new building in the fall of 2019. Classrooms are clustered in "hubs" of four teachers, with an open learning area in the middle that can be shared by the teachers in that hub. To accommodate the individual needs of students, there will be flexible seating in each hub that will give students a great deal of choice (exercise balls and wobble stools, for example, in addition to "regular" chairs). Each group of teachers, working with Principal Terri Myers and Assistant Principal Kathy Galford, has been able to make decisions around important norms that will guide the work of each hub (including, for example, the development of common routines and procedures). Each group is tasked with the final decisions as to a set of norms by which they will operate. The finalized norms may vary from hub to hub, but it is the teachers who finalized them, refining early brainstorming efforts into an agreed-upon set of guidelines.

Teachers and staff enjoy being part of the decision-making process when given the opportunity.

Teachers and staff enjoy being part of the decision-making process when given the opportunity. There is a great deal of satisfaction that comes from working together in search of worthwhile, student-centered goals. The energy that a group of teachers working as a team provides when in pursuit of the development of a school improvement plan, for example, can give rise to a great deal of synergy that improves the outcome. Every one of the teachers in each of Great Bridge Primary School's hubs brings a different set of perspectives that will improve operations and facilitate student progress. And when teachers are working on such projects, they must have clarity in terms of who is making the final decision. This clarity needs to be provided up front in the process as it was with Great Bridge Primary.

YOUR TURN

Confusion is the enemy when it comes to directions, procedures, goals, feedback, and performance expectations. In a classroom filled with 35 sophomores, there could well be 35 different understandings as to what the teacher intends. Teachers should constantly work on their own communication standards and must model what is expected when it comes to classroom expectations of any sort. Working the room is difficult enough without doing things—or not doing things—that will provide clarity for students who need to know what is expected.

REFLECTIVE QUESTIONS

Could you find a colleague—or several colleagues—willing to do a bit of research on what makes good, clearly understood feedback, then meet once a week or twice a month to discuss and digest the information?

Are there changes you can make when it comes to giving students directions that would avoid misunderstandings once an activity begins? (This has been a rule of thumb in my presentation work: If I want teachers to have a content-laden conversation in standing pairs, I give them one-at-a-time directions related to process before they know what they will be dealing with and discussing as it relates to content. When everyone is facing me in pairs, then we begin. I get the process out of the way first. Process first, content second.)

What are some ways to collect student feedback as to what was clear—and what wasn't—during class today (or this week)?

Are there ways you can use visual prompts to support organization and efficiency in your classroom? (Figures 6.1, 6.2, and 6.3 provide examples.)

CHAPTER

7

Making Time to Write

While observing in an elementary classroom one October morning, I watched as students opened their journals and began to write. As pencils moved busily over paper, the students hummed along with Vivaldi's *The Four Seasons* ("Fall"). This violin concerto from Vivaldi's most famous work played at a low volume and allowed just enough time (at a little under 5 minutes) for each student to make a short journal entry prior to sharing them with peers. As her students wrote, the teacher walked around the room conducting the occasional quiet conversation and letting students know by her presence (not at her desk grading papers) that there was nothing more important to her than what they were doing during those 5 minutes. Their body language told me they enjoyed making those short entries in what appeared to be dog-eared and much-used journals, and their teacher worked the room in an efficient and supportive manner.

Giving students opportunities to write takes a commitment in terms of time, and teachers who feel they have to move at warp speed through the curriculum may hesitate to pause long enough to allow students to write about what they think, then talk with peers about what they wrote. If we want our students—in any subject area—to understand and make sense of something we deem important, writing about it will do the job. The National Commission on Writing (2006) report makes the case for finding time to write: "If students are to make knowledge their own, they must struggle with the details, wrestle with the facts, and rework raw information and dimly understood concepts into language they can communicate to someone else. In short, if students are to learn, they must write" (p. 47). This is not rocket science. "If we want students to get better at reading and writing, they need to read and write a lot and think about what they are reading and writing," explain Harvey and Goudvis (2007, p. 36). Frequent opportunities to write on topics in any discipline help students understand the subject matter more deeply.

Frequent opportunities to write on topics in any discipline help students understand the subject matter more deeply.

Toward the end of my teaching career, my students—to whom I gave frequent writing assignments—often wondered aloud if I were an English teacher or a history teacher; I happily pointed out that in effect I was both. The Common Core State Standards make it clear that teachers in subject areas other than English language arts share the responsibility for helping students gain mastery in the area of writing. The report of the National Commission on Writing concluded that "although there is much good work taking place in our classrooms, the quality of writing must be improved if students are to succeed in college and in life" (p. 49). It is good to see writing return to center stage, and teachers in all disciplines should insert plenty of writing opportunities into the mix.

This has to be a collaborative effort as English language arts teachers work with colleagues in other subject areas on this continuous-improvement effort for students at all levels. Veteran teachers in social studies and science who may have gotten away from providing in-class or out-of-class writing opportunities can collaborate with English language arts teachers so everyone is on the same page in terms of mechanics and grammar. Students who are writing in three or four different classes will seek consistency when it comes to various forms of feedback. Teachers and administrators can take part in August professional development sessions devoted to writing so that students are not confused by three or four separate approaches to the *mechanics* of writing. Consistency across subject areas will benefit students who are tasked with writing more frequently than before.

We as teachers and administrators need to increase the quantity and quality of writing through the grades, and principals can insist that teachers in all content areas insert writing into their lessons. The benefits to students of being able to communicate well orally and in writing are tremendous. The results of a survey the American Management Association conducted of its members in 2010 included the percentage of respondents who look for communication skills (oral language and writing) when hiring: *81%!*

> *The benefits to students of being able to communicate well orally and in writing are tremendous.*

As a sales manager many years ago, I read hundreds of résumés from prospective sales representatives and had to discard a high percentage of these documents because they were so poorly written. I did not have a remediation program like many colleges, and this customer service job required excellent communication skills; as a result, I could not hire people who might otherwise have made good sales representatives. The same was true when I interviewed potential employees in person or over the phone. Anyone involved in sales of any kind deals with clients, and oral language proficiency is paramount. Speaking supports writing, and both kinds of communication are important in life and the workplace.

Speaking Supports Writing

Taking the time to discuss something with peers or with the teacher in a conference can set students up for writing. As we saw in Chapter 3, such conversations give students "a brief, but essential, chance to try out their ideas on one another, quickly solidifying their thinking before moving on" (Keene & Zimmermann, 2007, p. 41). Reading supports both academic conversations and writing, as it helps students develop new vocabulary. These three—reading, writing, and oral language—amount to the three legs that support the critical-thinking skills stool.

Tactical Tip

Working with students on grammar is everybody's business. A teacher in any subject area who recognizes patterns in the mistakes students make in their writing or when speaking can certainly take the time to deal briefly with these mistakes. The English Department can be notified as well, not as a way of placing blame on anyone but as a way of informing them about what the teacher is seeing in his or her essays and other written work. The development of literacy skills in the Common Core is referred to as a shared responsibility, another way in which teachers are all on the same team.

Students can make frequent entries in reflective journals and learning logs. Quickwrites can allow students to ping off something they just read. Teachers can follow a short lecture with time for students to reflect on what they heard, and after viewing a YouTube clip, students can take a few minutes to stand and talk with partners—and then write. Students can write and read their poems in class, getting feedback and encouragement from classmates along the way. Students can choose a topic dear to them and write about it. In short, there are many ways classroom teachers in all disciplines can help students learn to *enjoy* writing while simultaneously improving comprehension.

Online learning platforms provide teachers and students with the ability to post, edit, and self-edit pieces of writing. If writing checklists and rubrics are posted so they have easy access to these tools, everything students need is available after hours, and working the room for the teacher means spending some time each evening providing real-time feedback to students who may do a good deal more work at home than in the classroom.

Hooking Kids on Writing

Ask the kids in any second-grade class to raise their hands if they consider themselves writers (or artists or avid readers), and watch all the hands go up. Their world at that age is full of experiences that can be captured in words and pictures, and they are quite willing to share and record what they have to say, especially if they are provided with a great deal of latitude when it comes to writing topics. An elementary teacher who was going to be absent for a few weeks asked Shelley Harwayne (2001) to run her writing workshops while she was gone. Harwayne hit upon the idea of inviting those students—and all the students through Grade 5—to contribute to an anthology they would then present to the teacher Harwayne had temporarily replaced. She challenged them to write about things no adult could write about, and the kids were hooked.

They brainstormed possible topics and came up with things like sharing a bedroom with a new baby brother, getting braces, being teased on the playground, selling lemonade, having to leave school in the middle of the year, and scores of others. She challenged them, and the students "wrote enthusiastically, easily, and most of all expertly about topics most of them had never considered writing about before" (Harwayne, 2001, p. 7):

> Tactical Tip
>
> The iGen'ers who inhabit today's K–12 classrooms want lots of choice when it comes to just about everything. Instead of having all students write on the same topic, brainstorm with them a list of possible topics, then let them choose. I find it enjoyable to write for teachers, but I would find it painful—impossible—to write for an audience of nuclear scientists. If we want students to want to write and if we want them to really enjoy the process, then choice is important, whether they are writing essays or short pieces in their own logs (online or on paper). In classrooms with flexible seating arrangements, students can sit, lie down, or stand while writing.

> On this occasion, I think our students wrote well for a number of reasons. They relished the challenge. They owned the turf. They trusted that they had important things to say. They breathed the details. They delighted in the audience response. (Harwayne, 2001, p. 9)

Notice that everyone was not writing about the same thing. They chose the topics and went to work capturing their own experiences on paper.

Students who learn to love writing in elementary school should walk through the doors of middle school and then high school to find teachers in all subject areas encouraging them to develop the inseparable skills of thinking and writing. Reagan (2009) says, "*Deep and careful thinking before, as well as during, writing is necessary for deep and careful writing*" (p. 152). This means students must have the time to write in class, and this may mean displacing time formerly spent on lecture or other forms of teacher talk. One high school biology teacher made it clear to his students from the first day of school that they would write frequently in his biology classroom, and they did. Students who continue to write all the way through school improve their chances of landing a job in a global economy where communication and critical-thinking skills are becoming increasingly important.

Students who continue to write all the way through school improve their chances of landing a job in a global economy where communication and critical-thinking skills are becoming increasingly important.

At the secondary level, teachers can still provide a great deal of choice when it comes to writing assignments. Also, teachers can tap into the personal experiences of students as a way of engaging students in content. While the Internet provides students with much more information about topics related to immigration in the United States, for example, the initial *doorway* to the whole concept of immigration may be found in the following topics for a middle school student in a social studies classroom:

- Describe your thoughts as you anticipated a move from one school to another.

- Describe what you had to do when you moved from one community to another.

- What do you remember about your experiences when you arrived in this country?

- Explain what you left behind when you immigrated to this country.

- Describe what it was like to be the newest student in a classroom.

- If you were born here and lived in a foreign country for more than a year, what adjustments did you have to make?

- Describe the difficulties you encountered while learning a new language.

- Describe what it was like to adjust to a new neighborhood after your move.

- If one of the adults in your family lost his job, how did that affect you and your family?

- If you had to get rid of all but one suitcase full of your belongings before moving to another country, what would you keep?

- What would it be like to have to say goodbye for many years—or possibly forever—to a favorite relative or friend?

- If the amount of money you currently have to spend was cut by 90%, how would that affect you?

- How difficult would it be for you to find yourself in a community where almost everyone spoke a different language?

Tactical Tip

The list of writing topics I provided could be used in any history classroom or in a literature class. If you develop your own list of topics and want students to talk about a few before landing on a specific topic for their own writing, put them in standing pairs facing the screen, where your list is displayed. Give them this cue: "With your partner, talk about which of these topics interests you and why. You will have 3 minutes. Make sure each of you has an opportunity to share. Questions? Go!" Circulate throughout the whole classroom, listening in on the conversations. If the conversation surrounding one topic is particularly compelling, ask the student who gave the explanation if he would mind sharing what he said with the whole class later on. If he agrees, call on him once everyone is back to their seats or before they sit down, while it is still clear in his mind. You can do this with two or three students, actually, and it serves the purpose of getting students thinking—no more so than the students who are sharing. Talking is thinking, as is writing.

When I taught U.S. history at the middle school level, we lived in an area full of military bases, and the mobility rate of our student population was extremely high. Most of the prior topics would have resonated with our students, and rather than taking a strictly chronological approach to 19th-century immigration (as I did then), I would let students reflect on—and write about—their own personal experiences, letting them choose from among a wide range of prompts. The more choice students have, the more likely they are to find something about which they want to write.

Once students have had a chance to deal with one or more topics from this list that strikes a personal chord with them, the listing can be put on the screen once more, students can be put in pairs or trios, and the pairs or groups can be tasked with trying to figure out if, how, and why they all connect. Is there an overriding concept or subject under which all these prompts might comfortably reside? Instead of being told what they all have in common, students can talk with each other as they discover and discuss possible connections. The teacher could also have them work in these pairs or small groups to come up with questions they could ask the teacher, the answers to which would provide clues. This helps build interest in the subject of immigration without saying, "We're going to spend several days on the history of immigration in the United States, and I know you are going to love it as much as I do. Open your notebooks, and turn to page 873 in your textbook."

Let Students Be Teachers

As they write on one of these topics, students can talk with peers about their experiences, while providing encouragement as well as feedback in the area of structure and grammar. A formal peer-editing process can reduce the amount of editing teachers have to do, and it allows students to develop their own editing skills. When I was a middle school yearbook adviser, one rule in play for the writing of copy for the book was "three before me." By the time I saw the draft of an article for any section of the yearbook, it had been seen and edited by at least three staff members. Teachers who insist on being the only editors and feedback-givers in the room are short-circuiting the learning process; students learn a great deal when they teach someone else. We need to let them edit their own work, along with the work of others. This gives them practice at giving feedback and asking clarifying questions of the other writers in the room and helps build empathy as they honor their peers and the writing everyone is doing.

Teachers who insist on being the only editors and feedback-givers in the room are short-circuiting the learning process; students learn a great deal when they teach someone else.

Online learning platforms provide students with an opportunity to write for a much wider audience. Editing and revising can be done online outside the classroom; if it is a more formal writing process on this particular occasion, a checklist, rubric, and examples of the most commonly used—and abused—grammatical and stylistic constructs can be made available for students once they leave the classroom. If students come to understand that mistakes are just forms of feedback—and not personal—they are much more likely to accept and benefit from the feedback they receive from peers and teachers alike.

Learning Logs and Journals

Providing students with an opportunity to write in their own logs or journals is time well spent. Along with the obvious cognitive benefits of such quiet reflection, it gives students a chance to recover after being on their feet discussing something in pairs or small groups. Students who have been up and moving for a few minutes are the beneficiaries of increased blood flow and the release of neurotransmitters. My experience is that when the writing activity follows a period of movement and exercise, students are more focused and less lethargic than if one bit of seatwork follows another in short order.

Burke (2009) distinguishes between learning logs and reflective journals. The former are "short, objective entries that contain mathematical problem-solving entries, observations of science experiments, questions about the lecture or readings, lists of outside readings, homework assignments, or anything that lends itself to keeping records." Reflective journals allow students to comment, express their own feelings about something, "and connect what is being studied in one class with another class, or with life outside the classroom" (Burke, 2009, p. 112).

One Texas middle school teacher had her students write in their reflective journals after working in pairs or groups. The idea was to reflect on how well they worked together on that particular occasion. Did we all get a chance to contribute? Did we ask questions if we did not understand something? Did we use supportive body language and facial expressions? Did we take turns when contributing? Did we draw others into the conversations? There are tons of process-related questions students can write about—and then share with their teammates—as part of the continuous-improvement process as it relates to collaboration.

If we want students to process information after viewing a video in science, there are two things that will help: First, they can follow a short video on hurricanes and other powerful storms with entries in reflective-lesson logs (Burke, 2009, p. 112). This bit of reflective writing can be preceded by a stand-pair-share activity, where students get to process the information with peers. Or the reflective-lesson log entries can be followed by the conversations.

My suggestion is to have the stand-pair-share follow the video because it gets students up and moving between two seatwork activities. If students are going to write about what they have read, says Angelillo (2003), they need to "practice coming up with and rolling ideas around in conversation" (p. 20). If those conversations can take place while students are seated, they also can take place while standing. If students have been writing for a few minutes or if they have watched a short video and followed that with a period of written reflection, getting up gives them a break from sitting. The act of standing sends more blood to the brain, carrying glucose and oxygen; being able to move and talk for a bit is an added bonus.

Students can raise questions as well during the paired conversations, questions that can be dealt with by the teacher or by their partners. These conversations, along with the questions they surface, will combine with the video itself—viewed a few minutes ago—to provide context for journal entries. Either way, the idea is to have the processing (whether written or verbal) directly follow the video, lecture, or in-class reading assignment.

Reflective Blogs

Reflective writing captures where students are at any point in time, and utilizing reflective blogs allows them to go back and reference various progress benchmarks on one site. As with any kind of writing, exemplars are key. Before students can begin work on a reflective blog, they first have to know what a good blog looks like. As related in Almarode and Vandas (2018), fifth-grade elementary teacher Tanya Marchman-Twete and her students began their work with blogs "by asking students what they already knew about blogs and exploring kid blogs that were on the internet." On the second day, she opened the door to the whole idea of reflecting on academic-related work by talking about "what it means to reflect on one's behavior [a concept fifth graders know well]" (p. 92). This provided the foundation for both an understanding of what reflection is and what·makes a good blog.

After brainstorming "what metacognition looks like when reflecting on one's work" (p. 92), she and her students created a set of key elements (success criteria) against which students could check their own blog entries as they worked. As her fifth graders began using their reflective blogs, Marchman-Twete followed up periodically to see how students were doing, soliciting feedback on the process. The reflection extended not just to the criteria but to the whole process. Teachers who don't work on systems improvement may find down the road that it has broken down and is not being used because the reflection does not extend to continuous improvement.

The important thing here is that reflective writing, whether in a traditional paper-and-pencil journal or in an electronic format, provides students with ways to capture thoughts and check progress in real time as they reflect on both content and process. The very process of writing causes students to reflect on their own thinking, and my experience is that spending just a few minutes in a bit of reflective writing raises important questions, the answers to which will facilitate forward progress and ultimate success.

> *The very process of writing causes students to reflect on their own thinking.*

Connecting the Writing to the Writer

A student once explained to me how she survived high school. I'm pretty sure she was referring to the time she spent in the school building, not the time spent doing what interested her outside the confines of the many classrooms in which she sat in a mostly passive mode. In schools where students are relegated to the role of passive observers, Calkins (1994) says we see the energy of students "only in the hall and cafeteria, before and after our classes, and especially after school, when they are out from under our control and can pursue their own projects" (p. 172). The magic happens when we as teachers can find time during the school day to tap into what drives them.

A rich context for writing is created when students are engaged in many simultaneous discussions about various subjects that interest them in some way. In a fifth-grade classroom one afternoon, I asked the students what they were passionate about subject-wise, and one boy stood, threw his hands into the air, and said, "Dinosaurs!" Students of all ages have buttons that, when pushed, can get them talking, asking questions, sharing, deliberating . . . and writing. If we want students to be effective writers, the assignments can't always be about course content. If students are *always* asked to write about things with which they have little experience and little content knowledge, they may begin to see writing as something they don't necessarily want—or like—to do.

We are so concerned with mandatory testing and pacing guides related to curriculum that we may not take the time to help students develop a sense of inquiry; in our hurry to cover it all, we fall back on the time-honored tradition that Wolk (2008) calls the transmission model of teaching. There is little time in this delivery system for students to investigate, talk about, think about, and write about what really interests them. "Giving children time in school to inquire into topics and questions that they initiate may be the most important way to arouse wonder and passion in children and the will to pursue a life of learning" (Wolk, 2008, p. 122). Students are much more likely to want to write about that which interests them; too often writing assignments are made that have everyone marching lockstep through the same topic. My experience is that this turns kids off quickly, for the simple reason that they are not in any way interested in the topic. Inquire first—write later.

When I sit down to write, my brain invariably makes connections between what I want to convey and my personal life and experience. This is what the brain does; it makes connections. The stories of my life find their way into my books. When I think of something worthy of inclusion in my books, I write it down in a bid to capture what may be an otherwise fleeting connection to the material. Teachers who want to write turn to books for educators in the same way retired police officers often write police procedurals. It is familiar territory, and rich experience informs the writing process.

In the same way, the experiences of students will inform their writing for the simple reason that the connections are there—connections made possible by what they have read, heard, seen, or experienced in their own personal lives. Calkins (1994) recommends that students write often, and she applauds teachers who encourage students to "jot down things they notice and wonder about, their memories and ideas, their favorite words and responses to reading into a container of some sort" (p. 24). Calkins's "container" is the writer's notebook, but the name is not important. These journals or notebooks serve as "places for rehearsal. They are seed beds out of which rough drafts grow." Moreover, "when our youngsters begin the writing process by collecting bits and pieces—entries—in their notebooks rather than by listing and choosing among possible topics for writing, they are more apt to experience writing as a process of growing meaning" (Calkins, 1994, p. 24). I believe the best way to get students to love writing is to make sure they have plenty to write about that grows from their own experiences and their own learning.

Barbara Munza, a teacher whose work is highlighted in Harvey and Goudvis (2007), "asked her students to read and think about famous people who had made a difference in the world or who had overcome adversity or obstacles in their lives" (p. 191). One student read about Benjamin Franklin, then used a graphic organizer to record notes on Franklin's family, his interests and dreams, reasons he is famous, and other facts the student found particularly interesting. Synthesizing the information, the student then told the story of Benjamin Franklin *in first person*. As he learned more and more about Franklin, he *became* Franklin in passages that put him in the great man's shoes, including, "When I was 17, I decided to run away. I ran away to Philadelphia, Pennsylvania." Shifting from third to first person makes it personal, and the organizer with all the notes does indeed serve as "seeds" for the writing process.

Students of every age and description have personal experiences to share and stories to tell.

Students of every age and description have personal experiences to share and stories to tell. My experience is that when students are writing in class about something that allows them to tap into their own experience, the whole process moves along a lot more smoothly. Moreover, working the room for the teacher is a real pleasure for the simple reason that the students are not struggling or reluctant writers—and learners. Four decades in classrooms, including my own, also tells me students who are dragged through the system on a diet of "read Section 2 and answer the questions at the end" naturally build a resistance to having to write. Writing becomes a chore, not a pleasure. My suggestion to teachers today is to allow plenty of time for students to write about what interests them in ways that provide plenty of connections to their own experiences and their own knowledge base. If we want students to *want* to write and do so with growing skill, we need to think about how we as educators are going to facilitate this process.

Quickwrites

Having just read, seen, or heard something, students can take a couple of minutes to respond on paper. This is not a formal piece of writing but an attempt to allow students to capture their reaction to something on paper. Linda Rief (2003) has her eighth graders write every day:

> Quickwrites offer an easy and manageable writing experience that helps both students and teachers find their voices and develop their confidence, as they discover that they have important things to say. This quick exercise pulls words out of the writer's mind, and I am always surprised at the precision of language, level of depth and detail, and clarity of focus I hear when a student reads a three-minute quickwrite out loud. (p. 8)

Quickwrites may often provide the springboard for a more formal—and lengthy—piece of writing later on, but initially, they give students a choice by letting them respond to a line or idea from a short selection of poetry, prose, or other text. Rief believes quickwrites "encourage writing about important ideas, chosen to make us think and feel as we learn" (p. 9). The important thing about quickwrites—and all writing in all genres or subject areas—is that writing is thinking, and writing is learning.

Connecting Speaking With Writing

In her middle school science classes, teacher Kelli Marcarelli (2010) has her students use interactive notebooks "to make connections prior to new learning, to revise their thinking, and to deepen their understandings of the world around them" (p. 2). Students who can normally explain something orally can then use the interactive notebooks "as a tool to manipulate content knowledge, to integrate content with their personal knowledge, and to construct their own meaning . . . ." Her goal is to have them practice writing in a way that will make it "a pleasurable habit instead of an overwhelming task" (Marcarelli, 2010, p. 112). Marcarelli's subject area is science, but she understands that writing is not something that rests solely in the hands of language arts teachers.

In her science classrooms, Marcarelli is able to take advantage of the fact that her students can talk about and explain something, helping them transfer their thoughts to paper as they write in their notebooks. Zacarian (2013) reminds us that speaking, along with listening, is a great connection maker for students. "Actively engaging students in practicing what they will write by first talking about it," says Zacarian (2013, p. 104), is essential. Students who actively participate in paired conversations can literally discover what they think. From there, it is a short distance to recording these thoughts and understandings, assuming teachers give students the tools (interactive notebooks, reflective journals, learning logs) necessary to capture all this on paper.

For students, looking at a blank sheet of paper in anticipation of transferring thoughts into words is made easier if they have the opportunity to talk about the topic at hand first. Again, this is an active process that may have students standing and pairing with one or more partners. My experience is that working the room while students write is a lot easier for teachers if students are fresh from multiple discussions—and primed to write. If speaking supports writing, then it makes sense for teachers to set aside time for paired or group discussions *prior* to whatever writing activity is in the offing.

Confident Writers

When I visit classrooms, I look for two things: Are students engaged in meaningful work? How efficiently does the teacher work the room in support of that engagement? Walking into Jennifer Henry's fifth-grade classroom at Horizon Elementary, one is greeted by a dozen or more anchor charts hanging from clothesline throughout the room. These charts directly support reading and writing, and each of the anchor charts is the result of a collaborative effort between Henry and her students. Each 30- to 45-minute writing block is preceded by a minilesson where students discuss the topic at hand and create or add to the charts that are always accessible as they work. Figure 7.1 shows several of Henry's charts, which provide students with guidance and ideas.

Once students begin the writing process, time is set aside each Wednesday for small writing groups, where students can share their stories and receive peer feedback as part of the continuous-improvement process. Working the room for Jennifer Henry includes enlisting the support of her students in these writing groups, and the feedback Henry gets from her students reinforces this process. One student said she liked the writing groups "because I know how to change my story, and my group tells me what I should add to make it better" (personal communication, 2/1/13). Along these lines, Henry's students publish a class book every quarter that becomes part of the class library, and on the "Room 26 Authors" bulletin board, the stories are there for all to enjoy.

Figure 7.1   Anchor Charts

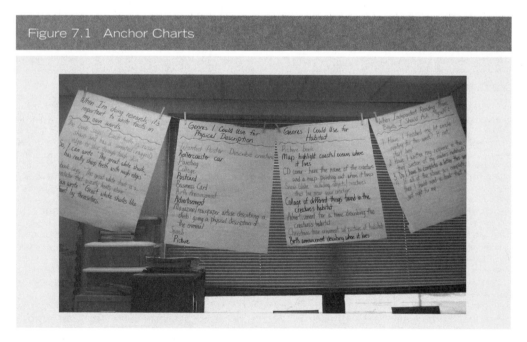

Source: Photo by Jennifer Henry.

Moreover, her students love reading what they wrote to the entire class. As one student said, "Why publish writing if you can't share it with people?" Why indeed.

Working the room for Henry is a collaborative process that ensures she is not on stage at every moment; she is not the automatic "go-to" person for her students. They are not dependent on her, and this is important. The anchor charts, myriad examples of student writing, and the feedback provided in the writing groups provide students with plenty of support they know how to access at every step in the researching and writing process. Jennifer Henry is not a walking checklist or rubric; the scaffolding she has put in place works to assist her students as they write and collaborate with peers. This efficient, supportive system guarantees Henry is not going to be exhausted at the end of the school day because she is not the one doing most of the work.

In Jennifer Henry's fifth-grade classroom, as in Kellie Marcarelli's science classroom, students have ample opportunities to write, receive valuable feedback along the way, share what they create—and become confident writers in the process. Writing is not drudgery; it is interesting and engaging work that takes place in classrooms where the teachers know how to work the room in ways that accelerate continuous improvement. Both teachers also understand the important connection between talking and writing. *Talking is learning*, and talking supports writing as students strive to become better at communicating, collaborating, and creating pieces of writing that are special and permanent.

Realizing the increasing propensity for students to cut and paste what they find on the Internet, inserting it into their own essays or papers without proper citations, it is my sense that more and more writing must be done in the classroom. Students who are confident writers are less likely to take another's work as their own. Teachers who encourage in-class writing of many kinds—using every formative feedback tool available—can facilitate the continuous-improvement process in ways that shift students along a continuum toward more confident and efficient writers.

YOUR TURN

If students are to become good communicators who can read, speak, listen, and write proficiently, we must provide plenty of time in the classroom for them to read, speak, listen, and write. Quickwrites and journal entries can help students capture their thoughts and develop ideas quickly. More formal written drafts should receive plenty of attention in the form of checklists and rubrics, along with peer- and teacher-generated feedback. Part of working the room for teachers is to make certain all these feedback pieces are in play. Teachers can enlist help from students and reference checklists and rubrics on the desks or in a laptop file as students work and use quiet conferencing to deliver information and ask questions.

In-class written work and outside assignments should tap into the experiences of students whenever possible. Writing of every sort (sentences, paragraphs, essays,

> *If students are to become good communicators who can read, speak, listen, and write proficiently, we must provide plenty of time in the classroom for them to read, speak, listen, and write.*

journal and learning log writing, and more formal assignments) should be included as part of in-class lessons, and plenty of examples of what makes a good sentence, paragraph, essay, or journal entry should be available to students in the classroom and online. In situations where it is possible, student work can be published in such a way that it can receive the kind of peer feedback that will help improve the process and the product.

As with any process, improvement in writing requires feedback of all kinds. Can you take the time to discuss the whole idea of feedback with your students? Can you brainstorm with them ways we receive feedback on a daily basis? (The most important thing about feedback is that it is the lifeblood of continuous improvement. Someone is likely to bring that up in paired conversations or in a whole-class discussion on feedback, and you can make sure it gets recorded on a chart or the whiteboard.)

When students are engaged in writing in the classroom, how can your time be best spent? (Not behind your desk, by the way. That sends this message: "Whatever you are doing out there is less important than what I am doing up here." Wrong message.)

How will you find time to move some of the writing that has been traditionally done outside the classroom into the classroom? (I found that by reducing the amount of teacher talk in my own classroom, I was able to set aside more time for in-class writing assignments.)

Considering the importance of mistakes and unforced errors in any effort or project, when will you approach with your students the whole idea of mistakes (and failure) as opportunities for improvement?

What opportunities can you provide for them to seek and receive peer feedback as they write?

8

Using Music to Facilitate Process

Several years ago, I spent 2 days in the seminar of a wonderful presenter. His timing was impeccable, and the seminar was informative and interactive. Time passed quickly, and it was difficult to leave at the end of the second day. He was as aware of the overall dynamics of an audience as anyone I have ever observed; he was an incredibly effective group facilitator. There was only one thing missing. As we went to and returned from breaks and as we moved into activities and paired up to process information, songs kept playing in my head: up-tempo selections; rock, rhythm and blues; and '60s pop tunes. What was missing was music. The timely and effective use of music would have made what was a great workshop even better.

I am aware that the teachers, administrators, and staff developers who read this book often provide professional development for colleagues in the form of workshops and seminars. In a 90-minute block, a 55-minute class period, a 2-hour seminar, or a 1-day workshop, music has many roles to play in our schools and in the professional development of educators. Therefore, in this chapter, I'll speak to those who teach students and to those who serve as presenters for the kind of professional development activities that support those teachers.

Music provides energy to classrooms and seminars. Music can also lighten up and energize faculty and committee meetings. Music can add just the right mood and create an atmosphere in which discussion thrives. The use of the right song at the right time brings smiles (and the occasional groan) to the faces of students and adult participants alike. Teachers who use music regularly in the classroom spend a great deal of time thinking about which songs might go with which activity or transition or about what song mix will serve to put an audience in just the right mood first thing in the morning or just after lunch.

Many teachers go to school quite early in the morning to set themselves up mentally for the day. And a good many presenters at conferences, seminars, and workshops show up early for the same reason: to prepare for what lies ahead by "reading" the room, checking sound systems and room temperature, arranging and rearranging desks and furniture, and choosing just the right personal attitude—all in order to increase the likelihood of success. Music is the perfect accompaniment to these prepresentation preparations. With a laptop, an iPod, or any MP3 player, teachers can set up a file of music composed of the songs that are guaranteed to put *them* in a great mood, something that is often essential in dealing with middle school students and adult learners alike. Listening to the music we love serves to put us in a great frame of mind for a day of instruction. It sets us up beautifully for the session, class period, or block.

Tactical Tip

Create a playlist or fill a CD with the kind(s) of music you love. Sprinkle your three or four favorite songs among the others; then, play it as soon as you arrive in your classroom in the morning. This will give you a dopamine rush that will help you focus and get you mentally ready for the start of the school day. Sing along if the spirit moves you. If you can listen to those songs in the car on the way to school, so much the better.

If music puts the teacher or presenter in a better frame of mind, the same can be said of students and seminar participants. Approaching a room where music is playing says that something different or unusual is going on in the room. Powerful teachers and presenters greet students and participants at the door to the room and circulate among those already seated, learning names and making connections, all to the accompaniment of appropriate music.

It is interesting to see how students (on the first day of school) or seminar participants (especially at an early morning session) approach the classroom from the corridor or hallway. If their expectation is that theirs will be a passive role and that the main mode of delivery will be lecture, music helps begin to change that expectation as it puts learners in a better frame of mind. They begin to think that this experience is going to be somehow different. That new expectation makes it easier for the classroom teacher or seminar presenter.

> *If music puts the teacher or presenter in a better frame of mind, the same can be said of students and seminar participants.*

I once had a seminar participant admit to me at the end of our day together that she came to the seminar anticipating "the same old thing," only to end up having a great experience—at least in part because of the upbeat music used during the course of the day. A middle school teacher told me that once she began using music at the beginning of every class, the number of students late to class dropped to zero in a matter of days.

When it comes to shifting moods from bad to good, Allen and Wood (2013) cite research that lists the top-four ways people accomplish that shift. The *top two* are exercise and music (followed by talking with a friend or loved one and trying to determine why we are in a bad mood to begin with). According to Allen and Wood (2013), "While research shows that the number one use of music is as a mood enhancer, using music to adjust one's energy level runs a close second" (p. 8). Most teachers in whose classrooms I spend time now use music in one or several ways, and I use it extensively in my workshops for teachers and administrators. The use of music never fails to lift moods and increase the energy level in the room.

Every veteran teacher or student can attest to the fact that even small distractions in the classroom can cause students otherwise involved in an activity to lose focus. Pencil sharpeners, the steady humming of HVAC units, coughing, sneezing, hallway noises, traffic noises, or someone mowing the lawn outside the classroom window—all these qualify as distractions to students engaged in some activity.

> The primary impediment to good, focused attention is distraction, in the form of all those novel, ambient sounds in the environment that call out to our stimulus-driven attention system. The goal of using background music is to cover these novel sounds so that they do not alert the stimulus-driven system to orient toward them, thus allowing focused attention to remain on task. (Allen & Wood, 2013, p. 96)

Working the room frequently requires teachers to have short, quiet conferences with individual students, and those, too, are distractions for the other students who are working quietly on an assignment. In classrooms where soft, instrumental background music is playing, I observe that students are much less distracted by other sounds or by conversations teachers need to have with students. The use of music in the classroom takes a great deal of planning to make it work effectively. What follows are a few more ways in which the use of music can enhance the classroom experience.

Music to Support Transitions and Breaks

It is necessary to give learners time to "unplug" and simply switch gears for a few minutes before turning to new material or changing to a new activity. This is as true in a 90-minute high school block as it is in a 2-hour session with adult participants. Even if a time limit for the break is announced, class participants may get involved in conversations and forget about the time.

Some teachers or seminar presenters will announce that the session will resume in 2 minutes and then give everyone a verbal 1-minute warning. This might serve the teacher well in a classroom where no one has left the room during the break, but in an adult-learning situation, it presents some problems. In an adult setting, where the participants have gone to use the restrooms or engage in a conversation in the hallway, not everyone hears the 1-minute warning. The first indication that the break is over may be when those in the hallway suddenly become aware that things in the seminar room have gotten quiet. Even those in the classroom present when the teacher announced the impending end of the break may have been so deep in their own conversations that they did not hear what was said.

Many teachers or seminar leaders will introduce a song (something highly recognizable and decidedly upbeat) and inform the students or seminar participants that when they hear that particular song, it is time to finish their conversations and return to their seats. When most of the participants are back in their seats (and while the song is still playing), one effective strategy is to pause the music and have everyone turn to his shoulder partner and say, "Welcome back!" Or if the next step in the learning process for that session is to turn to the textbook, workbook, handout, or binder, say, "Please turn to page 22 in your binder!" and give them some time to accomplish that. Meanwhile, the volume of that callback song can then be turned up and then cut off. The sudden silence gets the attention of an audience far better than anything the presenter can say or do (Allen, 2002, p. 85).

So far, then, I have suggested using music as preparatory to starting the class or as an attitude builder. The creative use of music for breaks can provide structure and save time, getting participants back on time and ready to go for the next session or learning module. Music can also be invaluable in the learning process as students and other participants interact with each other in pairs or in groups of three or more.

> ### Tactical Tip
>
> Students will ask if they can choose some music for transitions or as they enter or leave the classroom. A friend of mine, a high school biology teacher who used music all the time in his classroom, *always* listened to any song a student wanted played in advance, and he read the lyrics. If it was not appropriate, he did not play it. Any music used in any classroom must be appropriate, and teachers should be completely familiar with any song that will be heard by their students. If it isn't appropriate for *any* reason, don't play it!

Music to Enhance Discussions and Support Activities

It is no secret that some students and adult participants enjoy speaking in front of a group more than others do. Anyone who has spent any time at all attempting to facilitate conversations in groups knows that there are those who do not feel comfortable sharing with a large number of people, especially if it amounts to a solo act. It is much easier to use a strategy like Lipton and Wellman's (2000) paired verbal fluency (Chapter 4) to get students to engage in a structured discussion in pairs and then (later on) to increase the number of participants in the discussion group to three or four.

Another way to get everyone in the room involved in discussion is with a tried-and-true strategy like *think-write-pair-share*, a variation of the original *think-pair-share* strategy developed by Professor Frank Lyman and his associates at the University of Maryland. Teachers and other facilitators of group process are familiar with this interactive strategy, but let's see how it might be enhanced with the use of music.

Think-Write-Pair-Share

Most teachers don't hesitate to ask questions in the classroom. The problem comes when we try to wait any length of time for an answer. Waiting is not something teachers like to do. Indeed, we will often jump at the first hand that is raised, so anxious are we to get the "correct" answer. Every teacher and presenter has a "fan club" of those who seem to have all the answers, those who will respond at a moment's notice. If teachers are willing to work only with students who are quick to process, others who need more time to think will fold their cards early in the game. If this goes on regularly, then there are those in the class or audience who will permanently disconnect. These students and participants simply will not participate when they understand that time is rarely going to be available for them to process.

Rowe (1986) cites research that makes a case for providing adequate wait time. She concludes that "the quality of discourse can be markedly improved by increasing to 3 seconds or longer the average wait times used by teachers after a question and after a response" (Rowe, 1986, p. 48). I suggest teachers stick to open-ended questions that allow plenty of latitude in terms of answers and stay away from closed questions that allow for only one or two correct answers. Teachers then need to train themselves to wait, giving everyone a chance to process.

I rarely play any music at all during this phase of the strategy. There are, I have found, many students and seminar participants for whom music is too great a distraction during this *think* phase. I do know teachers who use Baroque music as a backdrop while their students are thinking. My best advice is for teachers to conduct this phase *with* and *without* music to see which works best.

Think-*Write*-Pair-Share

This next step facilitates "a shift from internal engagement to an external product which focuses the interaction, and which [the teacher] can use to monitor learning" (Lipton & Wellman, 2000, p. 86). The students now have the opportunity to capture their thoughts on paper. The teacher is active during this phase, traveling around the room, observing, and assessing understanding by reading what is being written.

Music can be added to this phase of the activity. My suggestion is that teachers stick to light jazz (Earl Klugh), piano music (Carl Doy or André Gagnon), or classical (Mozart) as background music, with the volume kept low. As stated earlier, the teacher's job at this point is to move around the room. This makes a remote a must so that the volume can be adjusted, if necessary, as the teacher circulates. When it appears that almost everyone has written all they are going to write, the volume of the music can be brought up and cut off quickly as a signal that the next step in the process is about to begin.

Also, for the teacher trying this for the first time, get some immediate feedback from the kids. If they are fine with it and the results of the writing phase are satisfactory, music can again be used to accompany this phase of the activity. If the feedback is not positive, don't use it. I have seen it used effectively for journal writing, and I have had teachers tell me they tried it and discontinued the use of music for this phase because of negative feedback.

Think-Write-*Pair*-Share

The thinking and writing phases are critical in giving precious minutes to those who need time to process, gather their thoughts, and then commit them to paper. How much any student or participant has written is less important than the fact that everyone has something to share with a partner in the next phase of the strategy. For this next step in the process, students and participants should work with one other person in order to share out loud what they have written. The music now changes from classical or light jazz to something more upbeat as a "cover" for the paired conversations. I suggest instrumental music here; songs with lyrics, I have found, distract students trying to discuss something with partners. Any number of upbeat tunes by the Glenn Miller Orchestra ("String of Pearls" or "In the Mood") or Duke Ellington ("Take the 'A' Train") will do nicely. They are upbeat selections, but there are no lyrics to get in the way. Also, the tempo of these and other similar songs is not frenetic or discordant in ways that would inhibit paired conversations. Other, more modern, upbeat music can be used to get students back to their seats.

Think-Write-Pair-*Share*

The first three phases of this activity serve as preparation for the final phase. In this last step, students and participants feel comfortable sharing with the entire group because they had a chance to *think* first, *write* down their thoughts, and then *pair* with one other person before moving on to what many human beings hate to do: speak in front of a group or audience. My experience is that the number of people willing to share *after those first three steps are successfully completed* increases significantly over the number who will share *without* this kind of preparation.

If students are going to share with the entire group and have not experienced success with this in the past, one way to overcome that is to circulate around the room during the *write* phase. Teachers can choose three or four

With many collaborative strategies, music can serve as a mood lifter and energizer.

really good written comments and ask each of the writers in turn if they would mind sharing a particular written entry with the entire group. If they say yes, the teacher can remember their names and, during the *share* phase, come back to them so they can share out loud with the class. Some may indicate they do not want to share, and that is fine. Make sure they understand you are perfectly okay with them not doing so. By choosing students who do not usually share with the group and knowing full well that what they have written down is a winner, they can perhaps finally taste something they may not ordinarily taste: success.

Clearly, although this strategy takes some time, it helps students build confidence; to those who normally don't participate because they don't process quickly, it provides time to think about the question or topic, write down as many responses or comments as they think they can, test their responses out with a partner under cover of some music, and *then* possibly share with the entire class. With many collaborative strategies, music can serve as a mood lifter and energizer.

The Role of Music in Choosing Learning Partners

Often, a teacher or seminar leader comes face to face with a situation where having people stand up, find a partner, and process information through discussion is desirable, even though it was not planned. A great time for this kind of random pairing is when teachers notice that students have been sitting for 10 or 15 minutes of direct instruction and need to process the information. In this case, the teacher can instruct participants to stand up, find someone with whom they have not yet discussed anything, and introduce themselves. Upbeat tunes ("Respect," by Aretha Franklin, for example) are perfect for getting students up and moving.

When everyone is in pairs or groups, the teacher can press the pause button and say, "With your partner or partners, please discuss . . . !" Once the instructions are complete, the music begins again, and the teacher circulates (with remote in hand or in pocket), giving some additional instructions when the time is almost up: "You still have 15 seconds." The volume then increases for a very short time, and the music is cut off. Partners are asked to thank each other and are instructed to move back to their seats (to the accompaniment of a new song).

> *Movement of participants within the room provides the perfect opportunity for the use of music that is extremely familiar to everyone.*

Movement of participants within the room provides the perfect opportunity for the use of music that is extremely familiar to everyone. If participants are simply moving from one location to another, the lyrics can't get in the way of productive thought. I have seen students and adults "groove" (rather than simply move) to their seats, ready to deal with whatever comes next.

Those upbeat songs can serve as cues, as is the case in Melissa Martini's fifth-grade classroom at Sanders Corner Elementary School (Virginia). When she wants students to pair up and review what was just taught in a minilesson, she plays a song that gets them to stand with a hand in the air, then pair with a partner somewhere in the classroom. Music then accompanies them back to their seats, which may be (their choice) exercise balls, wiggle seats, or swivel disks at standing desks. Martini understands the role of movement in learning. "Physical exercise increases two of the brain's neurotransmitters, dopamine and norepinephrine," writes Tate (2012), "which help to create a stable mood and assist in the transfer of information from short-term to long-term memory" (p. 72). Studies have shown that pleasurable music also aids in the release of dopamine, so movement and music provide a win-win situation in classrooms. Today's iGen'ers (Twenge, 2017) like plenty of choice, and Martini lets her fifth graders choose their own seats and partners in her classroom (personal email, 2/15/19).

Choosing Music

In *Top Tunes for Teaching: 977 Song Titles & Practical Tools for Choosing the Right Music Every Time*, Eric Jensen (2005b) identifies songs to go with every occasion in the classroom. For example, Jensen's (2005b) list of upbeat energizers includes "Happy Together" (The Turtles), "Shining Star" (Earth, Wind, and Fire), "At the Hop" (Danny and the Juniors), and "Do Wah Diddy Diddy" (Manfred Mann) (pp. 37, 43). These are all familiar tunes; students' parents or grandparents might listen to them, so the kids may have come into contact with them from an early age. An amazing number of songs from the 1960s and 1970s are showing up in commercials, movies, and television shows.

When I taught seventh grade, I used classical music as a backdrop for a study hall at the end of the day. I played mostly Baroque music, and Mozart and Vivaldi were regular contributors to the general atmosphere in that seventh-period class. One day one of my students raised her hand and reminded me that I had forgotten to turn on the music. I asked her what she would prefer and she responded, "How about the Vivaldi?" Once I recovered from the shock of a seventh grader asking me to play classical music, I asked her if she would prefer "Spring," "Summer," "Winter," or "Fall" from Vivaldi's *Four Seasons* composition.

Teachers who play different kinds of music are often planting seeds, albeit unintentionally. My junior high school music teacher used to play classical music for us at least a couple of times per week. We seventh graders grimaced, groaned, and otherwise resisted Beethoven, Mozart, Schubert, Rachmaninoff, and the other great classical composers. As an adult and shortly before that former music teacher passed away, I had the opportunity to thank him after he retired for hanging in there with us and with those great composers. He planted the seeds early, and I am forever grateful. One never knows when such seeds will sprout and grow, but exposing kids to all kinds of music may just widen their taste in music.

For those interested in reading more about music in education, Eric Jensen (2000b) speaks directly to "music's positive effects on the brain" (p. 1). Jensen (2005b) also provides examples of song titles that might be used for specific classroom uses and situations. The definitive volume on the use of music in the classroom may well be *The Rock 'n' Roll Classroom: Using Music to Manage Mood, Energy, and Learning,* by Rich Allen and W. W. Wood (2013). I highly recommend this indispensable resource for teachers, workshop facilitators, and anyone else who teaches or trains at any level. Allen and Wood have combed the literature for research on the effects of music on learning, and they have listed many hundreds of song titles teachers can use as students read, write, transition, take part in academic conversations, and clean up or line up. There are selections teachers can play to calm students down after recess or raise the energy level at any point during the school day.

Finally, for teachers looking for songs related to a specific theme or subject, Jeff Green (2002) has compiled *The Green Book of Songs by Subject.* This book lists more than 35,000 songs in nearly 1,800 subject categories. A science teacher doing some planning on a photosynthesis unit might discover some useful music related to the sun ("Walking on Sunshine") or the color green ("Bein' Green") that can be worked into the lessons. A double indexing system makes subjects easy to find. This resource is now available online, and those interested in locating songs about certain topics can visit www.greenbookofsongs.com.

Technology

New technology replaces the old with remarkable speed, and the CD players I used back in the day are disappearing. For teachers who still wish to use them, the CD player should be a top-loader that makes it possible to switch CDs quickly. Machines with multiple-disc capabilities slow down the operation when speed is essential. Speed and simplicity are necessary in multiactivity lessons or with strategies like think-write-pair-share. Being able to switch from one song to another quickly is important.

More and more teachers are moving to iPods and other music players that allow the creation of whole files for specific situations. For example, a file can be set up for use when participants or students begin to arrive in the morning. As participants come back from lunch at a seminar, a separate file can be used. Other files can be created for a whole set of activities related to a specific topic or for the morning or afternoon of an all-day session. A completely different file can be set up for use at the end of the seminar or class as participants mix with each other and exit the room.

An expensive sound system is not needed for classroom use, and discount stores sell iPod- or MP3-compatible units that would serve nicely. The key component is the remote; I always recommend teachers make certain a remote comes with whatever sound system they want to purchase. Teachers who use an electronic whiteboard to play music can have access to an unlimited number of songs, but the convenience of the remote is lost.

YOUR TURN

Teachers and students can benefit from the use of music. Those who incorporate music into their classrooms add a new and dynamic dimension to what may already be an excellent learning environment. Used effectively, music can help transform a classroom from passive to active in a short time.

REFLECTIVE QUESTIONS

Is there a think-write-pair-share activity in your content area that would allow you to practice using music?

In what ways can you use music in your classroom?

What songs might you select to accompany a celebration in your classroom?

What upbeat song would be perfect as the cue to get them into—and out of—standing pairs?

What songs might accompany a 2-minute exercise period?

Unlocking Doors With Storytelling

My favorite history professor had a gold pocket watch on a chain. When Dr. Haines removed that watch from his vest pocket and placed it in the corner of the large black desk in front of the classroom, then moved to a position at a front corner of the desk, we all sat back and relaxed in pleasurable anticipation of the story we knew was coming. He had the ability to tell wonderful stories that transported us to the Great Britain of another time. Kings and queens, prime ministers, philosophers, and other luminaries—and less well-known figures—came to life through the power of his stories. He used them to engage us and unlock doors into our imagination and into the material at hand. When he finished, we had questions, and he asked a good many of his own in order to flesh out the historical facts and concepts that formed the foundation for each story. Those powerful narratives were as highly anticipated by us as they were effective at opening doors to centuries past.

As a child growing up on the shores of Lake Erie, I spent hour upon hour outside, playing with all the other kids in the neighborhood a rather low-tech and extremely physical game called "kick the can" by its practitioners. One of us "guarded" the can while everyone else tried to be the first to kick the can without being tagged by the kid guarding it. There were other games (tag, foursquare, red rover come over) that gave us plenty of opportunities to dirty our clothes and reduce ourselves to a relative state of exhaustion in the process. The black-and-white television in our living room went unused for most of the day and evening during the summer and on weekends. The on-and-off knob and channel selector were both controlled by my grandparents, with whom I lived. That was fine with me; the action was in the yards of my friends on Gibson Street.

My grandmother read to me every night when I was of primary-school age, and my imagination got quite a workout before I went to sleep. Night after night, I created images in my mind, images related to the stories she told. Words were converted into pictures, and characters had faces as my imagination worked overtime at the end of a long day at school or at play. By reading to me on a regular basis, my grandmother did me an immense service. I still love to read and write, and the pleasure I received from those reading sessions in my early childhood jumpstarted those outcomes.

I don't claim that everyone growing up in the 1950s had this same experience, but there can be no doubt that there is a new reality for children today. Jensen (2007) reports that "the average child is watching media three to five hours per day (20–30 hours per week)" (p. 37). Cell phones rarely leave the side of iGen'ers, and Twenge (2017) writes in a book on that current generation that one of the police precincts in New York "recently warned residents about a danger lurking in their beds: their phones." They were responding to a growing number of fires caused by phones placed under pillows. A phone charging under a teenager's bed in Texas "overheated and melted into the sheets" (p. 49). Leaving aside for the moment that time spent looking at the screens on phones, computers, or televisions displaces time for play and other beneficial *physical* movement, this passive viewing also preempts "the developmental lack of imagination that demands full sensory, motor, emotional, and human interaction/intercommunication practice" (Hannaford, 2005, p. 75). So how do we get our students' imaginations off the bench and into the game?

The Focus Factor

For most of my teaching career, I spent entirely too much time in the classroom talking at my students and willing them to "pay attention." Sometimes, I would actually say, "Pay attention! This is on the test!" I had information to impart and little time in which to do it. I raised my battle standard (my black transparency marker) and cried, "Work with me here people!" Hardly a once-more-into-the-breach exhortation, I think you'll agree, but it was familiar territory for an embattled history teacher with a textbook the size of a small suitcase. If I wanted my students to focus, I just said, "Focus!" Seemed straightforward enough, if unimaginative—and entirely ineffective.

> *It did not escape my notice that when I took the time to tell a story tied to the content, I had my students' attention.*

It did not escape my notice that when I took the time to tell a story tied to the content, I had my students' attention. When I read a letter from a Civil War soldier to loved ones at home, everyone was with me, or, rather, with that soldier in 1863. Garmston (2019) affirms that psycholinguists refer to something called transportation, "when one loses oneself in the narration" of an effective story. Also, "hearing a story produces a neurochemical called oxytocin in the blood stream." This "enhances our ability to experience others' emotions." Oxytocin, says Garmston, is sometimes referred to as the empathy chemical, and it "motivates cooperation with others" (pp. 16–17).

As my grandmother and Dr. Haines understood, storytelling engages our minds in a way television can't. "Words shape how we understand ourselves and make sense of the world," writes Aguilar (2018). "Stories connect us with others past, present, and future; they hold our memories and pass on wisdom" (p. 70). According to Ollerenshaw and Lowery (2006), "Storytelling stimulates creative images about the world in the listener's mind. These images engage the listener during the storytelling experience and are interpreted by the listener as the story unfolds" (p. 31). By reading aloud to students, teachers certainly entertain, says Trelease (2006), and such stories also inform and explain. Combining an interesting story with the imparting of information is painless in a way that "telling" students things is decidedly not. When teachers read aloud to students, they also

- condition the child's brain to associate reading with pleasure;

- create background knowledge;

- build vocabulary; and

- provide a reading role model. (Trelease, 2006, p. 4)

A massive reading study conducted in 1990 and 1991 by Warwick Elley (cited in Trelease, 2006) assessed more than 200,000 students (9 and 14 years of age) in 32 countries. Among the conclusions as to what produced higher achievement in these two age groups was how often teachers read aloud to students and how often students were able to read for pleasure in school. (*Daily* sustained silent reading produced better results than that allowed only once per week. A North Carolina elementary school I had the pleasure of visiting years ago had the highest reading scores in the state; not coincidentally, perhaps, the principal mandated 30 minutes of silent reading every day. Students, along with every adult in the building, read what they wanted to read, not what was assigned.) There were other factors, but this is telling. In our rush to "cover" as much material as possible, we may discount—or discard—reading for pleasure and reading aloud to students.

Setting aside quality time for students to read for pleasure and reading to them frequently are important steps in getting them hooked on reading. The second step is to convince them that they are capable of telling stories themselves and, by so doing, developing *their own* communication skills. Reminding us that students like to talk about themselves, Marzano (2007) asserts that "one simple technique for engaging students and enhancing their level of energy is to create situations that allow them to talk about their interests" (p. 114). Glazer (2006) gives teachers a way to accomplish that by having students bring to school collections of objects they may have (baseball cards, stamps, stones, photos, etc.). The purpose is to get students to use their objects or collections as props as they talk about them. To get the ball rolling, teachers can begin with a very informal discussion on something they collect and, obviously, value highly. This provides a model for subsequent discussions and keeps it very informal. The idea is to "guide the children to understand that an object can represent an entire story" (Glazer, 2006, p. 86).

After doing this for a month or so, Glazer suggests moving from objects to words as the basis for student storytelling. The words (related to science, math, or any other subject) should "represent an event, theme, idea, or an object that facilitates storytelling" (Glazer, 2006, p. 87). Once the words are chosen and placed in a box,

> Setting aside quality time for students to read for pleasure and reading to them frequently are important steps in getting them hooked on reading.

Tactical Tip

A Virginia kindergarten teacher had her students on the rug in front of her rocking chair, and she had them divided into badger and bear pairs. She would read a portion of a story, then invite the badgers to retell that part of the story to their bear partners. She read a little more, then it was the turn of the bears to retell what they had heard. Rather than having one student, as is often the case, retell the story to the entire class, *she involved the entire class simultaneously.* They all got far more practice on these occasions than they would have had she not decided they should all be involved in the learning process. Understanding that time is a precious commodity, she used it wisely and to the benefit of her kindergarteners.

1. students are paired;

2. each partner selects a card from the box, without looking;

3. students look at their words and share their stories (based on the word) with their partner;

4. after telling the stories, students write them down (or draw them or both); and

5. students then use the selected word as the title and explain to the class why the story and its title are appropriately matched. (Glazer, 2006, p. 87)

The object, of course, is to build the communication skills and confidence of the students. Beginning, in this case, with something familiar (their own collection of objects) and moving eventually to subject area content (words related to that content) ensures that students don't have to tackle difficult content information before mastering the processes involved.

Opening Doors to the Content Material

Storytelling can be used "as an advance organizer, beginning your lessons or units with storytelling to engage students; storytelling serves to inform students about the purpose of the upcoming activity or concept, prompts questions, sparks thinking about the concept, and triggers connections with prior experiences" (Ollerenshaw & Lowery, 2006, p. 34). Once students are engaged in this manner, teachers can move into more unfamiliar and therefore more difficult material. In working with seventh graders on the U.S. Civil War, I approached the topic of abolitionism in the 1850s through a story from my own early adolescence.

First, I gave my students a short geography lesson that included the drawing in Figure 9.1.

I wanted them to visually understand how western Pennsylvania sits between Lake Erie and modern-day West Virginia. I also wanted to remind them that Canada is not too far across Lake Erie from my hometown of North East, a few miles east of Erie, Pennsylvania. Finally, I added eastern Ohio and southwestern New York to the drawing, along with the city of Pittsburgh. This whole "geography lesson" did not take more than a couple of minutes. To give them more time to digest the information, I would ask my Virginia students if there was anyone in the classroom from Pennsylvania, Ohio, New York, or West Virginia. There was always someone who had lived in one of those states, and it gave those students a close personal connection to the discussion.

Second, since our topic was the late antebellum period of U.S. history, I introduced a bit of historical context by pointing out that West Virginia was not a state prior to the Civil War. By explaining that what is now West Virginia was western Virginia in the 1850s and by adding that Virginia was a slave state and Pennsylvania was a free state, I was able

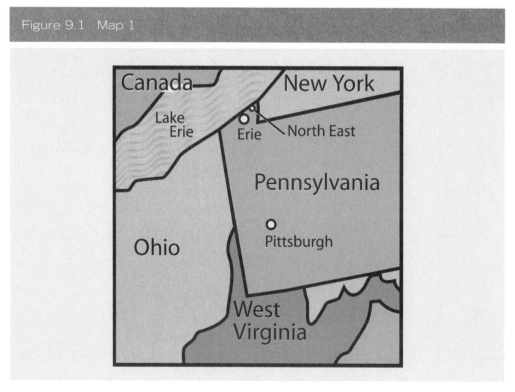

Figure 9.1   Map 1

Source: Brian T. Jones.

to begin shifting the students from the present day into that decade just prior to the Civil War. I pointed out that because slavery did not exist in Canada, many runaway slaves sought help in getting there.

Having delivered a very short geography lesson (based on the visual in Figure 9.1) and having followed that up with some historical context from the antebellum period related to the places on the map, I then told them the following true story.

One of the oldest houses in North East (see Figure 9.1) was across the street from where I lived. When I was in the sixth grade, a friend and I often played together in the house, which belonged to his grandmother. In the house was a trap door that led down into a short hallway opening into a secret room that contained two dirt benches with a dirt table in between the benches. Each of these benches was wide enough to seat two people, but there was not room to stand. Using a flashlight, we discovered an old lantern, a checkerboard (with checkers), and some wooden utensils, among other artifacts.

I can relate with utter certainty that I had my students' attention at this point. When I asked if anyone had questions, *they always did*. It took a combination of the map, some historical context, and the story to open the door to a deep and satisfying discussion of what that house was in the period before the Civil War: a station on the Underground Railroad. This allowed me to work into subsequent conversations the Compromise of 1850, the Fugitive Slave Law, Harriet Tubman, "Bloody" Kansas, Dred Scott, John Brown, and other people and events that were part of any discussion of the United States in the 1850s.

Ownership Through Questions

Earlier in my career as a social studies teacher in the 1970s, I used lecture and the overhead projector to uncover the sequence of laws, minor conflicts, and other relevant events that led to the outbreak of war in 1861. I have no doubt that, in spite of my best efforts, I did not get my students very deeply involved in the material. Conversely, when I first used the story of the Underground Railroad station in 1993, I was able to engage my middle school students and keep them engaged *because the moment they started asking questions, they invested in the outcome and wanted to know more*. The difference was illuminating, and once again, I was reminded of the power of storytelling firsthand.

Since that time, I have used the story with students and adults alike, and I have made a few modifications. At the point where I used to ask for questions (after telling the story), I now ask participants to turn to a neighbor and discuss questions they would like to ask *if they could ask questions of me*. After a couple of minutes, I record several of the questions on the board or chart *without actually answering the questions at that point*.

> At the point where I used to ask for questions (after telling the story), I now ask participants to turn to a neighbor and discuss questions they would like to ask if they could ask questions of me.

Here are some questions frequently asked by students and adults alike:

- For what was the basement room used?
- Why did the fugitives have to hide if Pennsylvania was a "free" state?
- Was the house a station on the Underground Railroad?
- Who owned the house in the 1850s?

- Did fugitives cross the lake? Where? When? How? With whom?

- Did the lake freeze in the winter? If so, could it be crossed?

- Were fugitive slaves finally free in Canada?

As stated earlier, when they begin to ask questions and discuss them with each other, the students are investing heavily in the eventual outcome, which is not only "what happened" in the story but also an understanding of the Underground Railroad, the Fugitive Slave Law, and much else related to the institution of slavery and the coming of the Civil War. When I start with the geography lesson (Figure 9.1), the material still belongs to me. The historical context (Figure 9.2) is mine. *By the time they ask questions and finish the story, they "own" the material.* This transfer of ownership from me to them is important because, with their interest piqued, I can now move into the content, safe in the knowledge that everyone in the room is along for the ride.

Nathanson (2006), after reviewing the research on its effect on teaching and learning, begins by saying that "story, or narrative, is a powerful—perhaps the most powerful—tool for teaching and learning because of its ability to hook audiences, activate the pleasure principle, and facilitate retention" (p. 2). He concludes that "recognizing the power of story and using it in the classroom gives teachers an effective teaching tool to promote active learning" (Nathanson, 2006, p. 20). That "hook" can serve to get students engaged in most subject area content.

I find it helpful when beginning a story to pause for a moment and look at the ceiling or off to the side. This pause, I believe, gives students time to adjust to

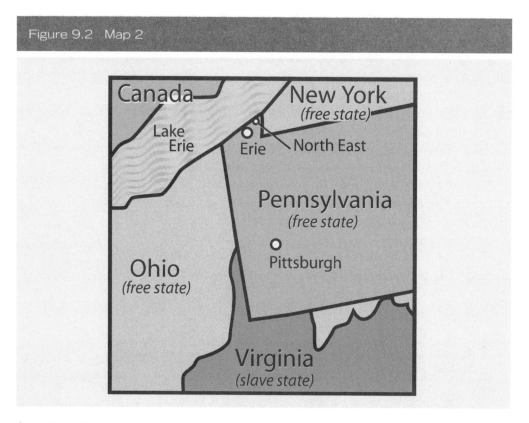

Figure 9.2   Map 2

Source: Brian T. Jones.

what is coming and builds anticipation. Lipman (1999) says that in normal conversation, a pause would invite the listener to reply or add to the conversation. An intentional pause during a story, however, "creates a powerful silence that may elicit eagerness, dread, or laughter" (Lipman, 1999, p. 35).

An extended pause at a crucial point in the story can serve as an opportunity for the teacher/storyteller to invite students to turn to a partner and predict what they think happens next. Once students have shared with a neighbor their own version of the story's outcome, the teacher can then ask a few students to share their theories. Then, the teacher begins the story again, repeating the extended pause and student conjecture once more before finishing the story. I have found that the anticipation built in this way at each pause gets students to invest heavily in the story's outcome and any point the teacher is using the story to make. Prediction is a powerful tool, and a story with a sense of mystery is perfect for this use of the mighty pause.

Tactical Tip

As it was with my college history professor who told wonderful stories to engage our imaginations and open doors to the course material, part of the pleasure of storytelling from the listeners' standpoint is the anticipation. That professor, Dr. Joel Haines, went to the corner of his desk and took out his pocket watch. That position by the desk was where he always told his stories, and as he established himself there, we were with him. We were ready. I tell teachers to find a captain's chair or a comfortable stool and place it near a corner and in a place where everyone can see you and from which location you can make eye contact with everyone. Settle in, turn your head slightly to one side, then turn back and begin your story. When students see the stool or the captain's chair, they know a story is not far off.

It's What They Think That Counts

Too often teachers feel they have to *tell* students stuff—the stuff of course content. We display a picture on the screen and proceed to tell students what they ought to see, what *we* see, or what is *worth* seeing. What's most important in our students' development as learners is not what *we* see, *but what they see*. Young children ask a ton of questions; they want to make sense of what they see, smell, touch, feel, and hear. As they enter school and move through the grade levels, we as teachers and administrators increasingly discourage questions because, after all, we know what students need to know—and time is precious.

> *What's most important in our students' development as learners is not what* we *see, but what they see.*

Gunter, Estes, and Schwab (1999) lament the fact that our current educational system institutionalizes "the departure from questions to answers as success becomes putting the right answer into the blank or circling the correct response, knowing positively what is true and what is false. Almost all questions in school have one right answer, and questions for which there are no answers do not often arise" (p. 122). But excellent paintings, music, political cartoons, diary entries, illustrations, and stories all serve to stimulate the senses and provoke the kinds of questions we once asked when questions were more important—and more frequent—than answers.

Paintings, drawings, and pictures provide insight into a period of time or a piece of literature—they tell stories on which words may not be able to improve. There are countless pictures from the 1930s in the United States (Dorthea Lange's breathtaking images come to mind) that elicit emotion and generate questions on the part of students who want to know more. These pictures are readily available to teachers, and they provide doorways into content—they *are* the content. Over the years, I have observed teachers who insist on explaining aloud what is in the painting or in the picture or in the political cartoon; let the *students* think about and talk with each other about what they see and feel as they observe the image. Ritchhart, Church, and Morrison (2011) provide an excellent and simple structure for students as they view something with which they are not familiar. It is called see-think-wonder, or STW.

STW begins with an image or object, a room full of students, and a commitment on the part of the teacher to allow time for students to observe individually and silently. The *see* phase of this strategy may involve a prompt that invites students to observe those things in the object or image on which they could put their fingers, assuming they could do so. This can be followed by a pair share, during which partners can talk about what they observed. The *think* phase of the activity is the interpretive part, where students can discuss with partners and then with the class what they think is going on with the object or image. The *wonder* phase involves asking students "what they are now wondering about based on what they have seen and have been thinking" (Ritchhart et al., 2011, p. 56).

There is structure here, but the search for a single right answer is not part of the equation. We want students to be observant, thoughtful, and careful thinkers. We want them to get into the habit of looking at something, at once pondering what they see and sorting out what it might mean.

I have found over the years that there is one powerful question that causes students—and adults—a bit of angst, taking them out of their comfort zones until they come to grips with it: "What makes you say that?" or, "What do you see that makes you say that?" or, "What did you read that makes you say that?" This invites learners to provide evidence for what they have concluded, and teachers should not be afraid to ask this question and then pause while waiting for the answer. With STW, Ritchhart, Church, and Morrison (2011) point out that asking questions like this "develops more considered responses, helping move students away from guessing or unsubstantiated opinions" (p. 56).

Here are some storytelling-related conversation topics for students in seated or standing pair shares:

- How does storytelling help with your understanding of a particular topic or concept?

- What do good storytellers do that keep you engaged in the listening process?

- What makes a good story?

- What story from your past or your experience would others want to hear?

Over the years, I have found that journalists often make great storytellers when dealing with history. Rick Atkinson is a case in point; he spent 20 years on the *Washington Post*, and he not only weaves a great story, he also enriches the experience by including the stories of others, thus tapping into the emotions of everyday people trying to grapple with sometimes extraordinary situations and life circumstances. In *The Day of Battle*, Atkinson (2007) makes us feel what the American soldiers felt as they moved into Sicily and up the Italian "boot" in World War II. This book is the second installment of a trilogy covering American involvement in that war, and all three volumes tap deeply into the experiences, fears, humor, and tribulations of the men and women who served on the European front, along with those who waited—too often in vain—for their loved ones to return. Their stories are an important part of the fabric of our history as a nation, and teachers can use those stories as doorways into the curriculum.

Students in social studies or literature classrooms who have the opportunity to read excerpts from letters and diaries—wonderful primary sources that convey emotion and help make connections that textbooks are not set up to impart—can be invited to draw inferences from these sources. They can then share those inferences with classmates in standing pair shares, at which point the teacher can invite questions to record and post on a class website or on an online learning platform. Finding answers to those questions can be the job of students armed with laptops, iPads, or their own computers at home. Remember, once students begin to ask questions, they are invested in the material. Questions provide ownership, and they are much more likely to want to find possible answers to questions *they* raised than they are to want to rush home and answer the ubiquitous questions at the end of the section or chapter. The stories of soldiers and the *relatives* of soldiers related in their published letters and diaries can open doors no dry textbook entry can.

> *Teachers who understand the power of stories and storytelling can harness it in the interest of learning.*

Teachers can use the stories of scientists, engineers, inventors, sports heroes, artists, musicians, authors, and countless others to open the doors to content. Once they get to know their students—including that for which they have a passion and a talent—teachers can point students in certain directions, increasing the possibility students will follow up on a suggestion concerning a certain author or subject. One Texas teacher gets to know her elementary students very well, and she also takes the time to read scores of children's books every year. When she is in the library with her students, she knows just where to send the student who seems lost because she knows which stories will engage those particular kids. Teachers who understand the power of stories and storytelling can harness it in the interest of learning.

YOUR TURN

Stories used in the classroom may be personal, told by teachers or students, or they may be resources selected as part of the curriculum. Personal stories are usually remembered because of our emotional attachment to them and because they do not tend to lose their immediacy or effectiveness over time.

Maguire (1998) provides a very good reason for sharing our own stories with others by informing us that "getting involved in developing and telling personal stories keeps us from unfairly dismissing large portions of our lives as boring, routine, or unremarkable" (p. 18). Every student has personal stories, the sharing of which may help build self-confidence—something of value not only in the active classroom but also in the workplace. Gewertz (2007) affirms that in the global economy, "it is not enough to be academically strong" (p. 1). Oral communication skills are an important part of the workplace equation today. Teachers can help develop those skills by providing opportunities for students to relate their own personal stories. The confidence they build may contribute directly to success in their chosen field. Simply put, telling one's own stories builds social capital and improves communication skills for students of any age.

Here are some ideas to increase the opportunities for storytelling in your classroom:

- As I did with the story on the Underground Railroad, consider using stories to open the door to content in a way that piques the curiosity of students.

- A personal story can be used to deliver feedback to a student or to the whole class.

- When trying to get students to understand that mistakes are opportunities for improvement, share one of your own stories about mistakes you have made.

- Students, in standing pairs, can share mistakes they have made, and you can ask for volunteers to share them with the entire class.

- Humorous stories can provide a mental state change for students, even if they have nothing whatever to do with the course content.

REFLECTIVE QUESTIONS

Can you locate a captain's chair or stool as a perch from which to read to your students?

Can your stories—or the reading of stories or parts of stories—be used to increase the number and quality of student questions?

Are there interesting stories or excerpts from stories that you can read to your students (of any age)?

What are some personal stories you can share in class that assure students that making mistakes is just part of the learning process? (And can you provide opportunities for them to share their own mistakes and unforced errors?)

10 Accelerating Progress

In my conversations with teachers whose students have achieved a great deal of success, they inevitably talk about taking risks and doing more as they seek to improve their own performance. If, as Winston Churchill said, failure is not fatal and success is not final, then teachers who continually take risks on behalf of those they serve will not be afraid to fail; they will use failure as a springboard. Great athletic coaches don't rest on their laurels or spend too much time celebrating after a win; the next game is not far off, and there is much to be done. There are mistakes to be made and unforced errors to overcome. For companies moving ever forward, iteration 2.1 awaits. For a sophomore, the second multiparagraph essay in his electronic portfolio can be demonstrably better than the last. And a self-reflective teacher, as we saw in the first chapter, can continue to make progress despite things that go bump in the road. Great teachers can express satisfaction but are never satisfied. Continuous improvement is a journey, not a destination.

Although I was involved in the development of a teacher evaluation system at one point in my career, I sometimes worry that such structures can be so cumbersome and time consuming as to get in the way of teacher improvement. Wiliam (2018) says he is often asked if he has research instruments for the purpose of evaluating teacher quality. "I don't," affirms Wiliam, "because working out which teachers are good and which teachers are not so good is of far less interest to me than helping teachers improve. No teacher is so good—or so bad—that he or she cannot improve" (p. 29). In the world of education, time is of the essence, and any time spent actively helping teachers get better and more effective at what they do is time well spent. One of my best friends, the late Kathy Hwang (Nash & Hwang, 2013), was a great principal in large part because she spent a large portion of every day in classrooms and with teachers and children. Continuous improvement was an obsession with Kathy because she understood what was at stake for her elementary students.

Much of what we do as educators should be in direct support of other educators as we all look to improve the learning process for kids. As it should be with students, "How did they do (summative)?" is less helpful for continuous improvement than, "How are they doing *right now* (formative), and how can we help *right now*?" My evaluations as a teacher (summative) mirrored my evaluations of my students (akin to a postmortem). I received a checkbox assessment once a semester, and I gave quizzes and tests that gave me grades for the gradebook. One principal required a minimum number of recorded grades per nine weeks. An obsession with formal, summative assessments can displace valuable time needed for a more formative approach.

> *Much of what we do as educators should be in direct support of other educators as we all look to improve the learning process for kids.*

Compliance-and-control classrooms like mine were replete with abrupt starts and stops in the form of grades and comments. ("I know you can do better. Hunker down during the new grading period!") "Grades can feel like stop signs to students," write Boss and Larmer (2018), "signaling that an assignment is over and done with. Formative assessment, by contrast, is all about what comes next in the learning experience" (p. 112). Too often, unfortunately for my students, they didn't get to "experience learning" at all. They were too busy getting ready for the next quiz or test. I reinforced this compliance-and-control approach by saying helpful (I thought) things like, "This will be on the test!" Their "experience" was limited to their role as passive observers and cramming for the next exam.

Reflecting on and increasing the amount of formative assessment—or summative assessment, for that matter—should not be backbreaking and lonely work on the part of individual teachers. It can—and should—be a collaborative approach. "Over time," writes White (2017), "collaborating and reflecting allows our practices to be more efficient and effective. Slowing down for a while means speeding up overall. Creating a collective clarity in our practice empowers us, as individuals, to invite change, creativity, and wonder in our shared classrooms" (p. 9). Efficiency, by the way, is not the same thing as effectiveness. My early classrooms were models of efficiency, but I was not ultimately effective in moving my students along on any sort of continuum toward a set of clearly understood learning goals. And I never opened the door of my classroom to other teachers, nor did I ask them to open their doors so I could benefit from what they were doing. I had plenty of energy, but it was directed at delivering information and a bit of entertainment on occasion. The synergy that comes from a collective effort toward a worthwhile goal was not on offer.

Marzano (2019) cites a good deal of research that "feedback—making students aware of their progress toward learning goals—is associated with an increase in student achievement" (p. 13). The types and uses of feedback can provide for a rich set of conversations in the summer, during the first week back for teachers, and throughout the course of the school year. Simple brainstorming sessions, followed by dialogue between and among colleagues, and some useful research on and examples of feedback used in the front lines can prove invaluable. Improvement is not possible without change; change requires feedback of all descriptions from myriad sources.

> *Improvement is not possible without change; change requires feedback of all descriptions from myriad sources.*

The Role of Feedback in the Continuous-Improvement Process

Multiple sources of feedback serve as the beating heart of improvement. Hattie and Clarke (2019) provide as complete an explanation of what feedback can do for students seeking to improve as any I have seen:

> Feedback is information about the task that fills a gap between what is understood and what is aimed to be understood. It can lead to increased effort, motivation or engagement to reduce the discrepancy between the current status and the goal; it can lead to alternative strategies to understand the material; it can confirm for the student that they are correct or incorrect, or how far they have reached the goal; it can indicate that more information is available or needed; it can point to directions that the students could pursue; and finally it can lead to restructuring understandings. (p. 3)

Feedback is all around us and comes unbidden much of the time. Running out of gas on the interstate provides immediate feedback concerning what is likely an unforced error on the part of the driver or drivers. My wife and I are obsessed with how our property looks, and neighbors whose dogs are walking them often compliment us on what they see as they walk past. In this way, feedback can be affirming. Also, as Wiliam writes, feedback can inform, motivate, and point us in different directions. It may lead us to say, "I used to think, but now I think . . . " as we restructure understandings. But it is an absolutely necessary and critical driver in the continuous-improvement process.

A football coach doesn't wait until the end of the game to provide feedback to his players or coaches. The feedback never stops, and it comes in every form imaginable, but to be effective, it must be received, and something must be done with it. Feedback that can be used immediately to improve upon a process or on performance is said to be formative. "To be formative," write Duckor and Holmberg (2017), "feedback needs to be used, understood, and processed by students to revise their performances so they can take another step toward the learning target" (p. 252).

In a classroom culture that encourages the giving and receiving of great gobs of feedback, improvements can occur quickly. My yearbook staff members met in my classroom after school, and those sessions were chock full of requests for feedback, particularly when it came to page design and the writing of copy. A copywriter might sit quietly for 20 minutes or more, then make the rounds in the room, draft in hand, to run something by another staffer. Award-winning yearbooks (which utilized the same standards we did) were spread all over the room, and the copy, photos, and page designs provided plenty of feedback for staffers engaged in continuous improvement. According to Duckor and Holmberg (2017), "Agreements and supports in the learning environment need to support reengagement so that revision becomes pervasive, even the norm, at school" (p. 253).

> *In a classroom culture that encourages the giving and receiving of great gobs of feedback, improvements can occur quickly.*

A high school physical science teacher told me her aha moment came when she realized she was not the only teacher in the room. Hers was a competency-based classroom where failure was not an option. Her students told me that they constantly provided—and sought—feedback from peers. In that high school science classroom and on my middle school and junior high school yearbook staffs for 4 years, the use of formative feedback in the interests of progress was the norm. Wiggins (2012) described formative feedback as goal-referenced, tangible and transparent, actionable, user-friendly, timely, ongoing, and consistent (p. 13). If revising student performance in any area is the goal, then formative feedback is a necessary accelerant in the improvement process.

A Clear Picture

The next time you are in your favorite supermarket (unless, of course, you access your favorite supermarket online and have your groceries delivered), walk down any aisle early in the morning, after the night crew has been stocking shelves in the wee hours. Chances are the shelves will look great, with all the cans, boxes, bottles, and jars standing at attention and on parade in aisle after aisle. Now, walk up to a can of beets, and take it off the shelf. If there is another can of beets right behind it and one behind that, the night crew did a proper job of what is called "facing" or "blocking." Repeat this with a bottle of juice, a box of cereal, or a can of cat food.

When in high school and at various points in my adult life, I worked in supermarkets, stocking shelves and bagging groceries. The owner/manager of the IGA where

I worked as a high school student taught us how to properly block shelves as we stocked them. To make sure the oldest items always got sold first, we stocked from the back of the shelf out. Any gap or space should be—and he modeled this for all new stockers—at the back. If he walked down an aisle and pulled a can off the shelf, there should be another can right behind it. That was the standard.

This standard of making sure the oldest merchandise leaves the store first (and doesn't get trapped against the back shelf forever) is in place in the industry because it is in the best interest of the customers who want food to be as fresh as possible. Stocking is a standard-based endeavor that takes time, concentration, and practice until a habit is formed. My job as the leader of the stocking crew was to make sure the standard was clearly understood and applied consistently. Veteran crew members would, as a matter of course, provide feedback for new hires unfamiliar with the standard or the process.

In the stocking of shelves or in the writing of an essay, learning goals should be visible and clearly understood by those expected to meet or exceed them. My car's GPS system works as intended only if I have provided a starting point *and* a destination. Anything less than that is likely to cause aimless wanderings and much frustration. The same is true of the learning process in classrooms. We want students to ask questions along their journey, says White (2017), "but it is impossible to ask questions to guide growth when we are unclear about the destination" (p. 94).

> When students are not clear about expectations or processes, their progress will be slow, hesitant, or nonexistent.

Confusion is the enemy for those expected to do the work and meet or exceed the standard in supermarkets or classrooms. When students are not clear about expectations or processes, their progress will be slow, hesitant, or nonexistent. In my experience—and I was guilty of this—when students are not making progress, teachers will sometimes play the blame game with colleagues in the faculty lounge: "These kids don't seem to have any energy. They don't want to learn." Teachers who are not themselves self-reflective and self-assessing may not realize the problem is likely not the kids.

When I was coaching regularly in classrooms, I would often spend a week or more in one school. This gave me the opportunity to see the same students in different classroom settings. Students adjust and respond to what is—or is not—expected of them. In a largely passive setting where students are basically attendees, Miranda goes to a better place in her mind as she watches the clock. In an interactive classroom where much is expected of her and where what is expected of her is clear and unambiguous, she rises to the occasion every day. Same kid. Different teachers. Very different cultures.

Which brings us back to the whole clarity issue, something a self-reflective teacher is constantly monitoring: "In essence," write Frey, Hattie, and Fisher (2018), "teacher clarity requires that the teacher knows what students need to learn, communicates those expectations to students, conveys the success criteria for students, and presents lessons in a coherent way. Teacher clarity is an important driver to improve student learning" (p. 16). Teachers who understand this are in a position to accelerate student progress. And students who understand the expectations and the success criteria are in a better position to self-assess, accelerate their own progress, assist and coach their classmates, and not worry so much about what is in the teacher's mind or what the teacher wants. If the standard is clear and the tools are within reach, students can confidently move forward as participants in—and drivers of—their own learning.

Bringing Students Into the Conversation

The whole notion of feedback in my classrooms was no doubt a mystery to my students, simply because I never took the time to explain the concept. I did not, as I might have done, engage them in a discussion about it. I had only the foggiest notion of what constituted effective feedback, and I constantly confused praise with feedback, thinking that "Good job!" and "Well done!" were pronouncements that were likely to somehow inspire students to hunker down and "work harder" in the pursuit of learning goals neither they nor I clearly understood. My job, as I saw it, was to come up with a never-ending series of quiz and test grades, record them in the gradebook, and send home the happy—or unfortunate—results of all that testing. Lather. Rinse. Repeat.

We are in such a hurry to "cover the material" in classrooms that we may not take the time to demystify continuous improvement as a concept. Students can engage in paired conversations on the *role* of feedback, along with the *types* of feedback; we can make them part of the conversation. We can invest time having students engage in paired, group, or whole-class conversations on the difference between—and uses of—formative and summative assessments. All this can lead to discussions about the impact of mistakes, unforced errors, and various obstacles on the improvement process. Students might be more cognizant of—and receptive to—all kinds of feedback if we took the time to lift the fog from an understanding of the topic.

> *Students can engage in paired conversations on the* role *of feedback, along with the* types *of feedback; we can make them part of the conversation.*

I believe students of any age know more about feedback than we imagine. One reason they don't add to and refine their understanding of the concept is that they are not asked. I had a supervisor who involved the whole office (20-plus employees) in a discussion of praise, including how we liked our praise—public or private. No one had ever asked that before, but what we discovered is that there were some of us who preferred whatever praise was headed our way to be delivered in private. Others did not mind—indeed preferred—public praise. She followed through on that, and we appreciated it.

She also encouraged feedback on her own performance, and someone told her that she had a tendency to continue to stare at her computer screen when one of us entered the room. She immediately adopted a new way of greeting visitors; she took her hands off the keyboard, swiveled her chair to face the door, and smiled, asking how she could help us. All this was much appreciated, and none of it would have happened but for the questions, the sharing, and the resulting, honest feedback.

Considering the importance of feedback as a facilitator of forward progress, it might be well worth the time to involve students in a discussion of the significant role it plays in the continuous-improvement process. Teachers and students can work "to collaboratively determine what kind of work is helped by feedback and what kind of feedback is the most appropriate" (Ruiz-Primo & Li, 2013, p. 220). It makes perfect sense that students who understand the importance of feedback to their own learning might well be more receptive to receiving it.

Tactical Tip

During the first few days of school, consider setting aside a sizeable block of time to have students discuss with each other two questions: Why is feedback important? What constitutes good feedback? Before putting them in standing pairs, they could do their best individually to answer these questions in a reflective log, then take the log with them as they meet with partners. They can take their pencils or pens with them to add to their logs as they talk. They can then change partners and continue the process, while you walk around, listening to the various conversations and, if warranted, asking two or three students to share with the whole group at the end. They can finish back at their seats by writing a few additional thoughts they may have hit upon when talking with others during the activity.

Any classroom observer can tell within a few minutes whether or not he or she is sitting in a classroom where the culture supports quality student-to-student interactions and, as part of that, peer feedback; in classrooms with a compliance-and-control foundation, such collaboration may well be unlikely. I have been in tension-filled classrooms where the negativity of the teacher has resulted in a culture that is inhospitable, much less collaborative. I have also observed classrooms where peer feedback is readily and frequently given—and is well received. In classrooms where it is patently obvious to everyone, even the occasional observer, that the social-emotional needs of teacher and students are not being met, feedback is not likely to be valued or accepted.

When I am in classrooms for even a few minutes, I observe the students carefully, gauging their general attitude and looking at body language. Where students are working in groups, I watch what happens when the teacher approaches a group. Either the students stop whatever it was they were doing as they look expectantly toward the teacher, or *they continue to engage as they were before they were approached*. In the first instance, the students may be looking for direction. In the second instance, my experience is that they are totally engaged in what they are doing, *and the teacher is just another learning partner in the process*. The teacher's visit is not disruptive. It does not make students anxious or put them on edge, as I have seen in some classrooms.

The state of mind of the students is of paramount importance. They need to be comfortable as part of a learning process that involves all of them in a collaborative, not competitive, environment. "When supportive and cooperative interactions in classrooms are the behavioral norm and when hostility and disrespect are absent, students report having higher self-esteem and feeling more intellectually competent and self-efficacious," write Rivers, Hagelskamp, and Brackett (2013). "In classrooms with more negative social-emotional interactions, students report a lack of nurturance and encouragement from teachers and are less motivated to participate and follow instructions in class" (p. 350). Like any plant or tree, feedback needs fertile soil to take hold and thrive.

> *Like any plant or tree, feedback needs fertile soil to take hold and thrive.*

In classrooms where I determine, even after a few minutes, that students are truly engaged in the learning (and not just in nominal groups, willing the little hand on the wall clock to move faster), the questions asked by a teacher when he or she engages with the group will have meaning—asking a student or a group of students what they have learned so far, what they will do next, or to explain something is meaningful and useful *only if the kids have been engaged in the work*. I asked a California eighth grader how what they were doing was relevant to the learning goal, and she explained it to me, without hesitation, in a way that demonstrated that she, her classmates, and her teacher had created a culture free of fear and anxiety and one conducive to forward progress.

Here are some questions students can ponder in seated or standing pairs, before sharing in a whole-class setting:

- Why is feedback helpful when we are trying to improve at something?

- What are some sources of feedback?

- Under what conditions are students more likely to receive and act on feedback?

Checklists and Rubrics

Going back for a moment to those early days of teaching when I increased the amount—and quality—of the writing I had my students do, it occurs to me that I was a *living, breathing, scurrying rubric*. It's no wonder I was thin then. As I hurried from desk to desk, students with their hands in the air had to wait until I arrived. This was as exhausting for me as it was crazy; I found myself explaining the same thing repeatedly—hardly an efficient use of my time. On occasion, I would interrupt everyone as they wrote, saying, "I'm getting this same question over and over. Please look toward the board while I explain it." Everything came to a halt at that point while I dealt with something I was sure I "taught" a week ago. In a 1970s world awash in superhero characters, I was *Rubric Man*. As I look back on it, I was also foolish; there was actually an alternative to this craziness.

Checklists and rubrics for almost any kind of project or writing assignment ought to be on every student desk or laptop, and they can also be made available on teacher websites for the benefit of students *and* parents. Easy access to these tools provides clarity—and allows teachers to make much more efficient use of their time during class. From the standpoint of a teacher whose time is precious because he or she is working a room with 30 seventh graders, checklists and rubrics reduce the number of basic questions students need to ask—and eliminate many or most of those waving hands and pleas for help.

The checklist tells students what needs to be done and in what sequence. It helps them "judge the completeness of their work so they know they are turning in what is required and are developing work habits in the process" (Brookhart, 2013, p. 18). Rubrics, conversely, assess performance. A rubric provides descriptions for various levels of performance. The rubric "*describes* the performance," according to Brookhart, in ways "that can be used for feedback and teaching" (p. 5). In my role as *Rubric Man*, there is no way I could have provided the degree of specificity provided by formal checklists and rubrics. Those two tools are extremely valuable for students who want to know what they need to do, along with what constitutes quality work. Together, checklists and rubrics provide clarity and reduce ambiguity and outright confusion.

> *Together, checklists and rubrics provide clarity and reduce ambiguity and outright confusion.*

This is not to say, however, that teachers need to disappear behind a mound of papers while students work at their desks, whether or not they have checklists and rubrics at the ready. I saw what I'm about to suggest used in an upper-elementary classroom, and it worked well: Students have one green and one yellow poker chip on their desks. As students begin writing, the green chip is placed on top of the yellow chip at each student desk. The green chip communicates to the teacher that all is well. As questions that can't be answered with the help of the checklists or rubrics arise, the student who needs help moves the yellow chip to the top; as the teacher works the room, he or she takes the wide view in order to see if there are any yellow chips. If there are two in view, the teacher puts one student on hold and moves to the next, letting the first student know he or she has seen the yellow chip and will be there shortly. This doesn't mean the teacher is going to stop only for yellow chips; it does mean the teacher can *first* deal with students who know they need help before visiting with others.

Again, the green chip says, "I'm doing okay here." The yellow chip says, "I have a question or need some advice." Here's a variation on this theme; a student who sees a yellow chip on the desk of another student can be empowered to leave what she is doing to attempt to help that student. This is not an abdication of the responsibilities of the classroom teacher; it simply acknowledges the fact that there are other "teachers" in the room, and their interventions may serve the purpose, providing clarity and direction. Allowing students to assist classmates adds to a sense of responsibility we are, after all, trying to encourage in students. This also frees the teacher to spend a bit more time with a student who needs that bit of extra help and guidance.

An online learning platform can provide the opportunity for students to edit and revise their work at any time; it also provides for more feedback from a wider audience. Learning platforms to which all their students have access provide teachers with somewhere to post examples of good writing—and good grammar. As students look for examples of the correct use of the apostrophe or subject–verb agreement inside or outside the classroom, teachers can help by posting such examples online. Anderson (2005) reminds us that our students do learn by example. "We have to flood students with elegant examples, whether it be decking the walls with them or individually collecting our favorite words, phrases, and sentences" (p. 23). We can cover the walls with examples and/or we can flood the online learning platform site with examples of excellent pieces of writing and grammatical usage that provide clarity for students at the click of a mouse.

Rubrics can have real value as students work in teams on projects as part of a PBL program. Having a clearly understood and familiar rubric at hand when needed can be a real boost for students. As her students engaged in a fourth-grade social studies project, teacher Abby Schneiderjohn, as reported by Boss and Larmer (2018), "used the same rubric for evaluating essays that students were already familiar with from writers' workshop. Students were able to use the rubric to revise their rough drafts and critique one another's writing during peer reviews" (p. 108). Rubrics can be cocreated with students, and there is real value in that because they get to unpack the learning goals; the connections are more easily seen by students when they are involved to this extent. Some rubrics are required by districts or developed as part of SIPs (school improvement plans). "Whatever the source, make sure that students understand the assessment language and know how to use the rubric to guide their growth as learners" (Boss & Larmer, 2018, p. 108).

Working the Room

I have often thought that teachers' desks take up more room than they deserve in classrooms. Sitting behind a teacher's desk while observing her classroom years ago, I noticed a coffee cup that seemed to have been there for many days—far worse when it seems as if the *teacher* has been there for many days, grading papers after students are "put to work" on various activities. Any teacher in any subject area who wants to accelerate progress on the part of his or her students simply has to work the room. Otherwise, students get the message that what *they* are doing is far less important than whatever is going on in the control room up front.

> The best teachers I know are true learning partners; effective and successful interactive classrooms include everyone in the learning process.

The best teachers I know are true learning partners; effective and successful interactive classrooms include everyone in the learning process, including the teachers and/or teacher assistants, who are on their feet and on the move. They glide from table to table and group to group, asking questions, taking questions, seeking information, probing for understanding, and doing a great deal more *listening* than talking.

They understand that listening is teaching, and they decrease the amount of teacher talk in favor of more student talk because talking is learning. This is why I learned more about U.S. history my first year of teaching than I did in 4 years of college; I did all the talking in my classrooms. I did the explaining, the describing, the elucidating, the illustrating, and the gesticulating.

Great teachers rarely sit behind their desks; indeed, many of them have gotten rid of them. While walking around one Virginia middle school classroom with the teacher, she admitted to me that her desk was little more than a repository for the flotsam and jetsam of teaching (binders, file folders, knickknacks, memos from August, and other ancient artifacts). The desk drawers were apparently where old pens, paper clips, and batteries went to die. She decided on the spot to get rid of the desk, along with some other superfluous items of furniture. It was a small classroom, and, again, this created more space for learning, rather than for storage.

When checking copy on my yearbook staffs over the years, I often moved around my classroom as my copywriters worked, asking them what they thought would engage the reader and provide good information and what they thought could use improvement. We used the same twelve proofreading marks used in the English classes at the middle school level, and staffers regularly utilized them to catch simple errors. Hattie and Clarke (2019) point out the importance of having students realize that mistakes are simply part of the learning process. This message can be delivered if teachers leave the comfort of their desks and work the classroom, encouraging, coaching, and asking questions. Left to their own devices, students who encounter problems and obstacles may simply give up.

One-on-one conferences with students allow those who might not ask questions or otherwise speak out in a whole-class setting to open up to teachers willing to hunker down next to them. Such conversations, affirm Stiggins and Chappuis (2012), offer teachers "an excellent context in which to provide specific descriptive feedback. Teachers can provide commentary on student performance and students can describe what is and is not working for them" (p. 273). One of the best biology teachers I ever knew used to walk around his classroom with a green pen while students were writing. He circled things that were done well. Notice, by the way, that he was a biology teacher, not an English teacher, but he had his students writing frequently in the classroom, where he could work the room in the interest of continuous improvement. His students, as I observed on more than one occasion, appreciated his frequent—and useful—visits to their desks as they worked.

One-on-one conferences with students allow those who might not ask questions or otherwise speak out in a whole-class setting to open up to teachers willing to hunker down next to them.

Jeff Bonine, a middle school science teacher at Health Sciences High and Middle College in San Diego, is constantly on the move in his classroom while his students work in groups. With the unit's learning goals firmly established in his mind, Bonine circulates, listening in on their conversations for the vocabulary and descriptions that tell him they, too, have internalized the learning goals and are making progress toward them. Working the room for Bonine "has always really been about trying to find out what the students are thinking, what they know, what their misconceptions are, and then using that formative information and prompting/questioning to help them bridge that knowledge with new learning" (personal email, 1/30/19). One of Bonine's goals is to have *them explain things to him* as he pulls up alongside one of the groups; there is a tendency for many teachers to do the explaining themselves in an attempt to "clear things up" for students. Listening carefully to student explanations tells him a great deal about where they are in the learning cycle, and all those interactions with individuals and groups better informs his instruction.

The best teachers and administrators I have met over the years have at least one thing in common: They are relentless in the pursuit of improvement for themselves and everyone around them in the schoolhouse. The finest principal I ever knew, the late Kathy Hwang, in a book she and I coauthored before her passing, wrote the following for fellow building administrators:

> Principals must seek feedback and work to ensure that those closest to the existing problems are involved in the solutions. Principals must have a sense of urgency, and everyone in the building, from the students to the adults, must know that steady forward progress, in every sense of the word, is a given—and is not negotiable. (Nash & Hwang, 2013, p. 12)

One of Kathy's favorite authors was Laurel Schmidt (2002), and one of her valued pieces of advice from Schmidt's *Gardening in the Minefield: A Survival Guide for School Administrators* was that the pressure to improve should be gently—but relentlessly—applied by principals. Kathy and I agreed that the same is true in classrooms. Teachers must be unquestionably committed to continuous improvement for students and for themselves. They must seek feedback at every turn and from every source. The best teachers I know are indeed relentless seekers of progress every day. Taking risks on behalf of children can help everyone get better at getting better. Going out on a limb can involve risk, but the end of the limb is where the fruit is.

YOUR TURN

As a young teacher, I found it was easier to provide information in the form of lecture than it was to try to navigate the rocks and shoals of getting students truly engaged in a culture of collaborative learning, where they would have necessarily taken some of the work load off me. I lurched into the weekend pretty much exhausted, but I'm sure my students, who had not expended a great deal of energy in my classroom, shot out the door like one of our cats when we open the carrier after returning from the dreaded visit to the vet.

"When the pressure is on," says Wiliam (2018), "most of us behave as if lecturing works, but deep down, we know it's ineffective. But leaving the students to discover everything for themselves is equally inappropriate. For this reason, I describe teaching as *the engineering of effective learning environments*." Moreover, says Wiliam, "The key features of effective learning environments are that they create student engagement and allow teachers, learners, and their peers to ensure that the learning is proceeding in the intended direction" (pp. 55–56).

Accelerating progress for students requires a culture of feedback that allows students to move forward without having to stand in line in front of the teacher's desk (as I have seen on many occasions) in order to get direction. Direction comes from peers, checklists, rubrics, multiple examples of readily accessible quality work, teacher visits at student desks and work stations, clearly defined learning goals, and countless small and spontaneous celebrations along the continuous-improvement highway. By serving as learning partners with students, teachers can continually inform their own learning and their own teaching as they participate in an interactive learning environment.

REFLECTIVE QUESTIONS

Mistakes and failure can help learners accelerate growth. However, students used to thinking mistakes and failure are bad—and as much as possible to be avoided—may not see it that way. Can you find time to explore (in paired, group, and whole-class discussions) the effect of mistakes and failure on continuous improvement? (Sharing personal stories of your own mistakes and failures should work to encourage them to share their own stories.)

Is there a colleague (or two or three) willing to take the time to regularly explore the uses of formative and summative assessments in the learning process?

How can you best create a culture of feedback in your classroom, and how can you involve your students in doing that?

How can you create opportunities for students to cocreate, with you, rubrics that will help them reach their learning goals?

Behind the Seen

Several years ago, a colleague told me this (true) story about a kindergartner on the first day of school. Mom paced near the front door of their home, waiting anxiously for her daughter to come home after that first morning session and finally spotted the school bus coming down the street. As the bus pulled up to the curb, she headed out the front door to greet her daughter as she disembarked. It quickly became apparent that the little girl was upset in the extreme, evidenced by the tears running down her cheeks. When Mom asked what was wrong, her kindergartner replied through the sobs, "They made us come home!!" I might have done that as a kindergartner, but I would remember if I did it in high school. I didn't.

At the urging of a principal, I settled myself at the back of a third-grade classroom near the end of a lengthy weather delay one snowy winter day. Soon students began to arrive, shaking the snow off their boots and placing their coats on hangers at the front of the room. The teacher greeted each of her students with a warm smile on that cold day, and some upbeat music accompanied their arrival. It wasn't long before the whole class of third graders was engaged in the learning process. It was obvious from the moment the first of those students entered the classroom that they loved being in that room—as did their teacher. I concluded quickly this was a professional who had invested considerable time and effort into building powerful relationships with her third graders. I stayed a bit longer than intended because I, too, loved being in that classroom.

The ultimate compliment for teachers may well be that students actually want to be there; *they like coming to those classrooms every day*. I have seen plenty of classrooms like this; students are so engaged that taking the time to go to the restroom is something to be taken care of quickly—otherwise, those kids might miss something. Two sixth graders told me they loved being in their language arts classroom; their teacher let them "do things." They were participants, not attendees, and they loved it. All this does not just happen, of course; it takes planning, persistence, practice, and patience. A considerable amount of quality groundwork was done by those teachers in the opening days and weeks of school.

It is not an exaggeration to say that what teachers do during the *first* 2 weeks *will determine largely how things go during the succeeding 34*. I can't possibly stress this enough. Anyone who spends any time at all in classrooms can conclude one of two things after just 30 minutes watching the teacher work the room:

> It is not an exaggeration to say that what teachers do during the first 2 weeks will determine largely how things go during the succeeding 34.

1. This teacher dedicated the first 14 days to creating a framework to support effective instruction.

2. She didn't.

She did, or she didn't. He did, or he didn't. It's that simple. When students are engaged and focused on a November day while the teacher glides from group to group asking questions, probing, encouraging, reinforcing, pushing, laughing occasionally, and taking care of potential discipline problems with a glance or two, an observer can safely conclude that the teacher put the process horse before the content cart early in the school year. The principal did not simply give the teacher all the "best kids" or the best schedule or the best materials or the best classroom; getting to the point where working the room is seemingly effortless takes a great investment of time and energy.

In this final chapter, we'll look at the first 2 weeks of school as a critical period that should be devoted to laying the groundwork for success down the road. In doing so, we'll add to, elaborate on, and occasionally revisit the environmental considerations in earlier chapters. We'll also tap into material introduced elsewhere in the book as it applies to those critical 14 days in August or September.

That Whole Groundwork Thing

Teachers often spend a good deal of time decorating their classrooms prior to the start of the school year; after all, every teacher wants students to walk through the doors of a classroom that is warm, colorful, and inviting. Nothing is wrong with this sort of preparation, as long as the teacher doesn't stand in the doorway of the well-embellished classroom on the last teacher's day before students arrive and draw the conclusion that after putting such effort into the decor, she is just one or two good lesson plans from a successful school year. I have never seen a laminated, colorful commercial poster that I could conclude had any effect—by itself—on instruction. Many wall posters have colorful cartoon characters exhorting students to "Respect others!" or "Do your best!" Classroom walls can be chock full of posters with rules, consequences, grammatical principles, procedures, catchy quotes, and the like; none of these carries much weight with kids who may not even *look* at them, much less reflect on them in a way that will affect their behavior or their performance.

If, however, those same posters are referenced regularly and made an integral part of the instructional processes in the classroom, that is, as they say, a different story. In one classroom, students working in groups ended their work together for the period or block by visiting a poster that had five or six collaborative norms against which the groups could, in turn, reflect on how well they worked together on that day. For students doing a good deal of writing in the classroom, a wall chart dealing with grammatical principles can serve a practical purpose. Wall- or ceiling-mounted visuals that are relevant, accessible, and easily understood can be useful as students work on projects or in-class assignments.

I would much rather see a classroom wall with six or eight permanent fixtures on which chart paper can be attached at regular intervals as teachers engage students in gallery walks. I enjoy walking into classrooms where the teacher has borrowed student artwork from the art teacher, creating vibrant walls covered with student creations. Precious and limited wall space can be covered with colorful graphics and photos that can be used as the centerpiece of reflective conversations and inquiry-based activities. As we saw in Chapter 7 (Figure 7.1), Jennifer Henry's fifth-grade classroom is replete with anchor charts hanging from clotheslines, charts developed with her students. Henry begins this process early every school year and productively uses every square inch of the floor, walls, and ceiling.

Teachers make many assumptions; this includes the assumption that commercial posters—by themselves—will have an impact. These assumptions, once made, short-circuit important questions that can impact teacher performance in positive and productive ways. None of us wants the family doctor to make assumptions about what ails us without making the time for gobs of reflection; we want our doctor to ask lots of questions, keep up with the latest research and literature from the field of medicine, and maybe even get a second opinion if necessary—*nothing less than our health is at stake*. If nothing less than the education of students is at stake, teachers need to question much and assume little, and in the days and weeks approaching the start of the school year, they need to read, reflect, and get a second opinion or two from colleagues as necessary.

Finding Time to Reflect and Ask Questions

All teachers can benefit from the collective perspectives and experiences of highly successful colleagues who have learned the importance of the first 2 weeks of the school year. It is also a safe bet that most problems and issues faced by any teacher or group of teachers have been faced, wrestled with, and otherwise pondered by others; the literature is replete with the experiences of teachers and tons of research. *Educational Leadership*, a highly respected ASCD educational journal, devotes each monthly issue to a specific topic, and teams of teachers could easily tap into this and other resources using a jigsaw activity. It remains for teachers, often working with administrators at the building or central-office level, to find out what is available in print or online that could help teachers plan lessons and work the room.

> All teachers can benefit from the collective perspectives and experiences of highly successful colleagues who have learned the importance of the first 2 weeks of the school year.

Teacher mentors and administrators can make certain *new* teachers do not enter the school year in the grip of false assumptions that can make working the room more difficult as the days and weeks unfold. Following are a few assumptions teachers—new or otherwise—may make as the school year approaches, assumptions that keep them from pausing, reflecting, and asking necessary questions. I'll highlight the assumption, provide some explanation, and raise appropriate questions that can be food for considerable thought and professional conversation during the summer months and throughout the year.

Challenging Seven Common Assumptions

Assumption 1: *Explaining my classroom procedures ought to be enough to ensure success during the course of the school year, especially if I have them displayed prominently on a large, colorful chart.*

Explaining a procedure is the beginning of a process. No coach ever explained his or her way to victory on Friday night or Saturday afternoon. If students are expected to walk quietly through the hallways, teachers must have them practice walking quietly through the hallways—and the expectation is best met if every teacher in the building is part of the decision related to hallway movement. This applies outside the classroom as well. I use my car's turning signal regularly for one simple reason: In my high school driver education class, my instructor had me use it regularly, until I didn't need his prodding. I don't get near the intersection today and think, *I am going to turn*

> Explaining a procedure is the beginning of a process. No coach ever explained his or her way to victory on Friday night or Saturday afternoon.

left, and I must therefore place my hand under the handle and push it down. I do it because the scaffold provided by my driving teacher was in place long enough for me to make using the turning signal a habit.

If students need to learn and correctly use classroom procedures (transitioning in an orderly way from student desks to standing pair shares, lining up safely and quickly before leaving the room, holding respectful face-to-face conversations with peers, or cleaning up efficiently and in a timely fashion after a chemistry lab), a scaffold provided by the teacher may be necessary until students do whatever is required without thinking. I know teachers who use a stopwatch or on-screen timers during the first couple of weeks, until students can perform a procedure in the shortest, safest way possible. One teacher has a series of transition songs (cleaning up, lining up, going from desks to standing pairs), all set to a 30-second limit. Students get used to getting to wherever they need to be, ready for whatever it is they need to do, in 30 seconds. For this teacher, 30 seconds is the standard, and the standard is achieved and maintained.

As we saw in Chapter 2, part of creating an environment conducive to learning involves turning procedures into routines (Wong & Wong, 2005) in ways that facilitate the continuous improvement process for students. Anyone mentoring new teachers would do well to reflect on the importance of process by asking and allowing teachers to reflect on all this. Following are a few relevant questions worthy of some individual or collaborative reflection before the school year begins:

Here are some planning-related questions that can be dealt with individually or collaboratively with one or more colleagues:

- What procedures must be explained, practiced, and adjusted during the first 10 days in such a way that they function in *support* of working the room and not *against* it?

- When these procedures begin to break down (and they may), how will I react? (Hint: Playing the blame game does not serve the cause of continuous improvement.)

- Is there an advantage to having a schoolwide leadership team look at procedures related to common areas of the school (hallways, cafeteria, play areas) with an eye toward consistency and safety?

- If I am one of several subject-specific teachers on a larger team, should we get together and decide on a basic set of procedural norms we will all use and support?

The bottom line here is that incoming fourth, seventh, or 10th graders, although new to their grade at the end of August, have been in scores of classrooms in their careers as students; indeed, they are veteran students who, for the most part, want things to run smoothly and efficiently. The teacher who wants to work the room successfully for 180 days must work to eliminate ambiguity and confusion when it comes to process. If students are expected to perform up to the standard when it comes to procedures of every description, teachers need to do more than declare the rules, demand compliance with them, and then refer students to the poster before moving into course content. Teachers must be willing to invest time and effort on *process* before shifting to *content*.

Assumption 2: When I'm ready to have my students shift from individual seatwork to pairs, trios, or quartets, as covered in Chapters 3 and 4, all I need are a few simple rules and all will run smoothly.

The whole idea of cooperation in support of a common goal seems so simple, yet anyone who has spent any time at all working with teams may readily admit that effective collaboration is not easy. As Johnson, Johnson, and Holubec (1990) affirm, "Switching a classroom from an emphasis on individualistic and competitive learning to a classroom dominated by collaboration is a complex and long-term process" (p. 135). The most successful teachers I have observed over the years have made a transition—over time— from students sitting in straight rows doing individual seatwork to students working effectively in small groups in classrooms configured for effective interaction.

Individual or collaborative teacher reflections:

- During the first 2 weeks of school, what can I do to increase the likelihood of success when I want students to engage in productive and ultimately successful collaborative work?

- To what extent do I need to help my students develop powerful social skills that will help accelerate the improvement process when they collaborate?

- What are some content-free conversations students can have in pairs (seated and standing) that will allow them to practice the kinds of basic listening skills they will need when working in small groups later on?

- What online or print resources will help me become a better facilitator when students are collaborating?

Resources that deal with adult collaboration and teamwork can inform the practice of teachers working with students. In *Unlocking Group Potential to Improve Schools*, Bob Garmston and Valerie von Frank (2012) speak to multiple levels of messaging that are part of basic communication: "When the social level message (usually in words) says one thing and the psychological message (usually reflected in voice tone, use of gesture, or emphasis) indicates something else," the psychological message will carry the day in the conversation (p. 5). The priority put on body language and tone is true of students as well, and the first 2 weeks of school is the time for a discussion about what we say and how we say it, and the problems that come from the two (often incompatible) messages we send in our discussions with other people.

If students—and their teachers—are going to succeed in creating and functioning in a collaborative classroom, the first 2 weeks of school offer plenty of time to explore the whole idea of listening skills and their importance to effective communication. When students stand together in pairs, one partner can take certain actions to let the other know he or she is listening. Appropriate eye contact (staring at someone is not appropriate eye contact) is important, along with positive body language and supportive facial expressions. Part of listening is asking questions when appropriate, as well as summarizing and paraphrasing in the interest of clarity and understanding.

The Common Core State Standards clearly support collaboration and comprehension under the speaking and listening portion of the English Language Arts Standards that also highlight the importance of oral language skills in the learning process. Participating in collaborative conversations, taking turns, asking questions during extended conversations, speaking audibly and expressing ideas with clarity, and following agreed-upon discussion rules—all these components of active listening and speaking are in the standards *for kindergarten*. In states where the Common Core State

Standards are in play, I suggest teachers take a close look at these standards for speaking and listening, regardless of what subject they teach.

To the extent that students in districts around the country do not come to the classroom ready to collaborate in any meaningful way, teachers must spend the first 2 weeks getting them ready to do so. Teachers should also model the same excellent listening skills they want students to master. A poster on the wall that tells kids *not* to interrupt is of no practical use if the *teacher* constantly interrupts. Third graders who see their teacher listen to their comments and questions with a furrowed brow and crossed arms will mimic this kind of dissonant behavior when meeting in pairs and groups. Teachers who want students to paraphrase effectively must model paraphrasing constantly. Working the room is difficult enough without the complication of a disconnect between the words and the tone of voice, body language, and so forth.

> *Working the room is difficult enough without the complication of a disconnect between the words and the tone of voice, body language, and so forth.*

Assumption 3: *Students are used to responding quickly to cues on the part of teachers; I don't need to spend time working on things as simple as getting their attention.*

Working the room is going to be a whole lot easier for teachers who can bring students back quickly and efficiently when they need to add something, ask a question, ask for *student*-generated questions, or get ready to transition to something else. Students should come back relatively quickly, but I would add a word of caution. If we ask students to talk about something in pairs or small groups, we must naturally assume that when the teacher wants to get their attention, students are in different places in their conversations. The teacher who wants his or her students' attention should also *honor* them by encouraging them to finish their sentence or thought before thanking their partners and turning to face her. Teaching students to transition between group activity and focusing on the teacher requires patience, and teachers should realize that as students get to know each other better and as they become more comfortable participating in these academic conversations, they will—and should—take a bit longer to recover, thank their partners, and turn.

Some teachers give silent cues. A few years ago, I watched as a teacher raised her hands (palms forward) and pointed both hands toward the rug in the corner of the elementary classroom. The kids stood, pushed in their chairs, and walked to the rug. She then joined them as she sat on a short stool in front of the now-seated class. The effortlessness of organizing the students did not happen by accident; she practiced that transition with them until they had it down. Allen and Rickert (2010) provide some suggestions for what they call "get-quiet cues":

- Hold two fingers in the air

- Hold hand up in the air, spreading out your five fingers

- Stand in a certain section of the room

- Hold one finger to your lips

- Hold hand up horizontally and gradually chop it down

Allen and Rickert (2010) point out that it doesn't matter what the silent cue is, but it should be practiced until it works every time, and it should be, well, *silent:* "No matter how frustrating it may seem, do not speak once you've made the cue. Once you say,

'Hey guys, this is the quiet cue,' the whole point of a silent cue is lost" (p. 99). Working the room is much easier without introducing myriad, possibly ambiguous ways of getting the attention of the entire class.

Here are some teacher reflections related to recovery cues:

- What *single* recovery cue will serve to get the attention of my students every time, regardless of what they are doing?

- Is this process something I can time, with an eye toward continually reducing the amount of "recovery time" during the first 2 weeks?

- If I am part of a subject- or grade-level team, can we agree on *one* recovery cue so that when students move from teacher to teacher we are being consistent?

- Would we as a faculty benefit from adopting a single cue in every classroom throughout the building? How would we accomplish that?

Assumption 4: Providing students with an auditory set of clear, multistep directions up front will suffice.

As we saw in Chapter 6, giving too many directions at one time may well cause considerable confusion on the part of students as well as frustration on the part of teachers who insist on giving those instructions in bunches. One middle school teacher gave her directions en masse, then spent at least 10 minutes walking around her classroom undoing the damage as she answered multiple questions related to process, opened books for students who should have had them open already, and probably wondered how she managed to get all the clueless kids. Had she given the directions one at a time, she could have avoided the confusion, the questions, and the Tylenol at the end of the day.

As a rule of thumb, I have found success by getting all the process-related directions out of the way first. Teachers can deal with each of these individually, in step-by-step fashion:

1. "Wave at your Blue Jay partner." (wait and make sure everyone has a partner)

2. "Stand behind your desk." (wait until the chairs are pushed in)

3. "Take your reflective journal off the desk and hold it in one hand." (wait)

4. "In a moment, when I say go, take your journal and meet with your Blue Jay partner somewhere in the classroom." (wait until you are fairly certain all students are with you)

5. "Go." (wait while the students transition, which should be quick and efficient if such transitions are now routine)

6. "Stand with your Blue Jay partner and face me." (wait until everyone is looking at you)

7. "Open your journal to the page on which you made your reflections this morning." (wait)

At this point, the teacher can give any further directions; each student should be with a partner, standing (with their journals), facing the teacher, and ready to go. I also recommend any directions beyond this point be posted on the board or listed on the electronic whiteboard, for reference as the students work. If prompts are used, teachers should ensure they are clear. Again, modeling may be a necessary part of this.

Assumption 5: *Students who do not understand something will ask questions.*

Some students would rather be locked in a room with unrelenting elevator music than admit they don't know something by asking a question in front of what they may see as a "jury" of their peers. Gunter, Estes, and Schwab (1999) put it this way: "Because few students want to announce their ignorance to the world, the request 'Raise your hand if you don't understand' is usually an ineffective diagnostic. Questions such as 'Are there any questions?' are hardly better" (p. 72). As a new teacher, I threw out the "Questions anyone?" line and got few hands. My interpretation of this reaction on the part of my students was that I must have done an outstanding job of lecturing for the past half hour; otherwise, questions would have been forthcoming in droves. The idea that my students had long ago traveled to another place in their minds, even as they looked me straight in the eye while smiling, never occurred to me.

> *The idea that my students had long ago traveled to another place in their minds, even as they looked me straight in the eye while smiling, never occurred to me.*

One reason students don't immediately respond when teachers call for questions is simple: They have not had time to reflect on what they just saw (video), heard (lecture), read (short reading selection), or wrote (reflective journal). It takes time to reflect on something and then formulate questions. Teachers are typically in a hurry to cover the material and perhaps stay in step with the pacing guide provided by the district. This focus on "getting things done" may result in little time for processing the material or raising the kind of questions that might come out of such reflective moments. Also, the students may well *know* the teacher is in a hurry, and they may get used to moving from this topic to another without much—or any—processing. Students are nothing if not perceptive, and if current practice in the classroom involves, "Are there any questions?" as an obligatory, auditory follow-up to a period of direct instruction, students may wait the teacher out in hopes that *this too shall pass quickly*.

When we as teachers say, "Do you have any questions?" we assume students are clear as to what they do and don't know about something they just saw or heard. In asking the question, the teacher is attempting to check for understanding, but as Fisher and Frey (2007) remind us, "Students aren't always self-regulated learners. They may not be aware of what they do and do not understand" (p. 1). If we want students to ask quality questions, we need to give them time for independent or interdependent reflection.

The appearance of meaningful student-generated questions may have to wait until students can connect new information with what they already know and perhaps until they have the opportunity to learn from the connections made by peers in academic conversations. At the point where many teachers throw out the, "Any questions?" line, students have only their own thoughts and experiences to fall back on, "but with lots of conversation," according to Zwiers and Crawford (2011), "a classroom has a wide range of experiences and connections upon which to build new learning" (p. 19). Students who spend some time writing in their journals and talking with peers about the material are in a much better position to ask questions.

> *Students who spend some time writing in their journals and talking with peers about the material are in a much better position to ask questions.*

Even if students have the opportunity to process information for a while, many may be unwilling to ask whatever questions they might have, simply because they don't want to ask something their friends might think silly, unintentionally funny, or irrelevant. If teachers eliminate these kinds of negative reactions on the part of classmates, more students will be encouraged to ask questions in pursuit of clarity and a deeper understanding of the subject. Something I have found particularly helpful in getting students to ask questions involves having students stand in pairs and share questions they might have with a classmate. Then, the teacher asks for volunteers to share what their *partners* asked: "Eddie just told me . . . " or, "Liz explained to me that *she* thinks . . . " To successfully participate, students must listen to what their classmates are saying. I first saw this approach used in an elementary classroom, and it worked beautifully.

Taking these questions as part of working the room must be a relaxed process and should not be rushed. Teachers who seem in a hurry cheapen the exercise, and students are less likely to share if they think this is all just window dressing. Pausing and paraphrasing come in handy as well, and students should become accustomed to this slowing down. The purpose of student-generated questions is to reveal understandings and misunderstandings and elicit even more questions. Students need to understand that it is okay not to know, and living and dealing with ambiguity is simply part of life.

We *want* students to be puzzled, and, when they get the chance to process the information, even briefly, according to Walsh and Sattes (2011), they "begin to wonder about it, . . . formulate a question, and then . . . begin to try to answer it" (p. 116). For teachers, part of working the room is to know how to keep the ball in the air long enough so that more and more students get the opportunity to make connections, juggle possible answers, and arrive at some conclusions on their own or with classmates.

A bit of teacher reflection that could be part of collaborative discussions before school starts as follows:

- How can I increase the number of questions—open and thoughtful questions—students ask?

- What are examples of open and thoughtful questions?

- How do I make room for more student-generated questions?

- What kind of classroom environment encourages student-generated questions that are spontaneous—not solicited?

- How does wait time make a difference after asking a question and/or after getting a response?

- What constitutes an excellent teacher-generated question?

- What is the best way to handle questions (pauses, body language, facial expressions, quality of responses, for example)?

Administrators could work with teacher leaders and within the context of the school improvement plan to conduct a book study or give pairs of teachers the task of reading the literature on topics like those surfaced in the list of questions posed earlier. As part of the process, teachers can use strategies they in turn discuss with colleagues as part of a concerted effort to increase quality as it relates to the whole concept of questions in the classroom. The first 2 weeks of school can offer an opportunity to begin using what surfaced from early discussions in August. Teachers can also invite colleagues into their classrooms to observe and provide feedback as the school—or at least a grade-level or middle school team—wrestles with this important topic. I recommend the book *Thinking Through Quality Questioning*, by Jackie Walsh and Beth Sattes (2011), as an excellent place to start.

Assumption 6: *If I want my students to collaborate effectively, standing or seated, whatever furniture configuration I inherited from the room's previous occupant will probably suffice.*

As we saw earlier in the book, certain classroom arrangements facilitate movement and sharing, and other configurations hinder them. Teachers should take the time during the week before school to decide what furniture arrangement (including bookcases, the teacher's desk, tables, and file cabinets) is conducive to moving and sharing and, by so doing, keeping the energy level high.

Here are a few reflections concerning furniture configuration:

- Will having students spread all over the room when standing create problems when I work the room as I observe, listen, and check for understanding?

- When students are seated, can they easily talk with a shoulder partner or face partner? If not, how can I create a configuration that makes my having students turn, face a partner, and process information at any time possible?

- Can I, alone or working with colleagues, come up with several configurations that could be used during the course of the school year, depending on what instructional strategies are being used?

- Is there furniture in the room that serves no instructional purpose and could be given away to colleagues or stored somewhere?

The bottom line here is that the furniture arrangement should support instruction—not cleaning. This is not to say teachers should take a confrontational approach when dealing with custodians. Every teacher in the school should strive to develop excellent working relationships with the custodial staff, especially the person who actually cleans his or her room at the end of the school day. I took the time to get to know the staff when I was teaching, and my extra effort paid off for the night custodian and for my students. I asked her what I could do to make her job easier, and we settled on several things I would make sure were in place when she walked into the room after school. Our arrangement included letting her know what I wanted kept on the blackboard (someone must remember blackboards) and making sure my students and I left the room in good order. Today, I would ask my custodian to work with me on various student desk configurations, in return for which I would once again make sure other things were done in support of the goals of the custodial staff.

Assumption 7: *I'm the only teacher in the room.*

In an elementary classroom where students were split into groups working on a variety of things, one group of four students sat reading for fun. One student tapped another on the shoulder and pointed to a word in his book, saying, "What does this mean?" His friend said, "Read the sentence to me." He was doing what all of us do in that situation; he was looking for contextual clues. When that didn't work, they opened the small dictionary on the quad and found the word. "Does that make sense?" said the reader's friend. It did make sense, and the student who had requested his friend's assistance thanked him, at which point they both returned to their reading.

Classrooms are full of situations where students could turn to the teacher for help or, not wishing to take it that far, just continue reading or writing without coming to grips with something they want to understand. The most successful teachers I know encourage students to help each other and do so for the simple reason it is not about the answer—*it is about the kids.* It is about helping make them independent and interdependent learners, and part of that is empowering them to help classmates.

Fourth-grade teacher Tracey Bennett "does not expect to be the only teacher in the classroom" (Johnston, Bennett, & Cronin, 2002, p. 156): "There are times when I am trying to teach something, and I have just run out of ways of getting it across effectively. I am very comfortable saying, 'Do me a favor. Go over to Elsa and talk it over with her. Come back and let me know what you guys talked about'" (Johnston et al., 2002, p. 156). Bennett also encourages students to share their entries in their writers' notebooks, and they love sharing and helping each other. "'I've got a bunch of resources right at my fingertips—my students. I don't have to try to come up with everything'" (Johnston et al., 2002, p. 155). Teachers don't have to be walking, talking dictionaries, checklists, rubrics, or explainers-in-chief; my experience is that students enjoy being part of the learning process by shifting into teaching mode frequently. The whole process of explaining or describing something helps *both* students understand the topic or concept more clearly.

One of the reasons I love standing pair shares is that students get to talk with a partner, reason things out, share things their partners don't know, or help them with things they may not understand. If students, as part of active listening, are taught to ask questions and paraphrase in search of understanding, teachers don't need to be part of the think-aloud process in order for teaching and learning to occur.

Final Thoughts

One thing powerful and effective teachers have in common is that they sweep away obstacles and remove barriers that can all too often serve as excuses for not getting the job done. They move inexorably forward and take no prisoners. My most effective teachers and professors over the years were those who were consistent, positive, fair, relentless, and loved being with us every day. They were willing to admit mistakes and had a sense of humor that underlined both their humanity and their sense of being human.

One thing powerful and effective teachers have in common is that they sweep away obstacles and remove barriers that can all too often serve as excuses for not getting the job done.

I often talk about my favorite teachers. In every case, when I recall those teachers, they were the ones who told stories, and they had us tell *our* stories; when I tell *their* stories, I remember every detail of the rooms in which they taught. I remember where I sat. I have total recall of the myriad ways in which they demonstrated their mastery of the profession. There was, in the final analysis, *something in them* that saw *something in us,* and this intangible but very real trait is one that characterizes great teachers through the ages.

The interactive classroom is a place and state of mind where students are engaged fully in their own learning, with teachers as learning partners. The new reality of the 21st century is that many of the jobs these students will hold require teamwork, interaction, conversation, and collaboration. Students who spend a good deal of time watching a screen of one size or another need also to be involved in structured conversations in our classrooms. This means they need to become proficient at the kinds of academic conversations that make them confident communicators. It is necessary for them to learn how to speak and write with confidence and *listen* with respect, empathy, and understanding.

To any outside observer, the energy is contagious and the learning visible in genuinely dynamic, interactive classrooms. In a safe and supportive environment, students can regularly pair, share, laugh, and learn while working on projects and other collaborative tasks. Teachers who approach groups in feedback-rich classrooms don't bring the proceedings to a halt; they listen, ask probing questions, gauge whether or not students know where they are in relation to where they are going, and look for an answer to the question, "Where to next?"

That question can be asked of teachers as doers, risk takers, experimenters, and tinkerers. Teachers can regularly pair, share, laugh, and learn while traveling together on the continuous-improvement highway. "Where to next?" can be a constant, benchmarking refrain for teachers willing to open their doors and engage in collegial efforts aimed at shifting all the learning partners in the school community toward a clear, shared vision. Working together can be far more rewarding than going it alone.

And it's more fun.

Notes

Notes

Notes

Notes

References

Abeles, V. & Rubenstein, G. (2015). *Beyond measure: Rescuing an overscheduled, overtested, underestimated generation*. New York, NY: Simon & Schuster.

Aguilar, E. (2018). *Onward: Cultivating emotional resilience in educators*. San Francisco, CA: Jossey-Bass.

Allen, R. (2002). *Impact teaching: Ideas and strategies for teachers to maximize student learning*. Boston, MA: Allyn & Bacon.

Allen, R. (2008). *Train smart: Effective trainings every time*. Thousand Oaks, CA: Corwin.

Allen, R., & Hann, M. (2011). *Humane presentations*. Moorabbin, Australia: Hawker Brownlow Education.

Allen, R., & Rickert, C. (2010). *High-five teaching, K-5: Using green light strategies to create dynamic, student-focused classrooms*. Thousand Oaks, CA: Corwin.

Allen, R., & Wood, W. W. (2013). *The rock 'n' roll classroom: Using music to manage mood, energy, and learning*. Thousand Oaks, CA: Corwin.

Almarode, J., & Vandas, K. (2018). *Clarity for learning: Five essential practices that empower students and teachers*. Thousand Oaks, CA: Corwin.

Anderson, J. (2005). *Mechanically inclined: Building grammar, usage, and style into writer's workshop*. Portland, ME: Stenhouse.

Angelillo, J. (2003). *Writing about reading*. Portsmouth, NH: Heinemann.

Atkinson, R. (2007). *The day of battle: The war in Sicily and Italy, 1943–1944*. New York, NY: Holt.

Bailey, B. (2001). *Conscious discipline: 7 basic skills for brain smart classroom management*. Oviedo, FL: Loving Guidance.

Bender, W. N. (2012). *Project-based learning: Differentiating instruction for the 21st century*. Thousand Oaks, CA: Corwin.

Bissell, B. (1992, July). *The paradoxical leader*. Paper presented at the Missouri Leadership Academy, Columbia, MO.

Blaydes, J. (2004). *Thinking on your feet* (2nd ed.). Murphy, TX: Action Based Learning.

Bluestein, J. (2001). *Creating emotionally safe schools: A guide for educators and parents*. Deerfield Beach, FL: Health Communications.

Bosch, K. (2006). *Planning classroom management: A five-step process to creating a positive learning environment* (2nd ed.). Thousand Oaks, CA: Corwin.

Boss, S., & Larmer, J. (2018). *Project based teaching: How to create rigorous and engaging learning experiences*. Alexandria, VA: ASCD.

Boynton, B., & Boynton, C. (2005). *The educator's guide to preventing and solving discipline problems*. Alexandria, VA: ASCD.

Bracey, G. (2006). Students do NOT need high-level skills in today's job market. *The Education Digest, 72*(4), 24–28.

Bradberry, T., & Greaves, J. (2009). *Emotional intelligence 2.0*. San Diego, CA:

Brookhart, S. M. (2013). *How to create and use rubrics for formative assessment and grading*. Alexandria, VA: ASCD.

Brooks, R., & Goldstein, S. (2004). *The power of resilience: Achieving balance, confidence, and personal strength in your life*. New York, NY: McGraw Hill.

Brunner, R., & Emery, S. (2009). *Do you matter? How great design will make people love your company*. Upper Saddle River, NJ: Pearson Education, publishing as FT Press.

Burke, K. (2008). *What to do with the kid who . . . Developing cooperation, self-discipline, and responsibility in the classroom* (3rd ed.). Thousand Oaks, CA: Corwin.

Burke, K. (2009). *How to assess authentic learning* (4th ed.). Thousand Oaks, CA: Corwin.

Calkins, L. M. (1994). *The art of teaching writing*. Portsmouth, NH: Heinemann.

Collins, J., & Porras, J. I. (2002). *Built to last: Successful habits of visionary companies*. New York, NY: Harper Business.

Conzemius, A., & O'Neill, J. (2006). *The power of smart goals: Using goals to improve student learning*. Bloomington, IN: Solution Tree.

Conyers, M., & Wilson, D. (2016). *Smarter teacher leadership: Neuroscience and the power of purposeful collaboration*. New York, NY: Teachers College Press.

Costa, A. (2000). Describing the habits of mind. In A. Costa & B. Kallick (Eds.), *Discovering & exploring habits of mind* (pp. 21–40). Alexandria, VA: ASCD.

Costa, A. (2008). *The school as a home for the mind: Creating mindful curriculum, instruction, and dialogue*. Thousand Oaks, CA: Corwin.

Costa, A. (2012). Intelligent behaviors. In P. Senge, N. Cambron-McCabe, T. Lucas, B. Smith, J. Dutton, & A. Kleiner (Eds.), *Schools that learn: A fifth discipline fieldbook for educators, parents, and everyone who cares about education* (pp. 240–249). New York, NY: Crown Business.

Davis, H. A., Summers, J. J., & Miller, L. M. (2012). *An interpersonal approach to classroom management: Strategies for improving student engagement*. Thousand Oaks, CA: Corwin.

Dennison, P., & Dennison, G. (1994). *Brain gym® teacher's edition revised*. Ventura, CA: Edu-Kinesthetics.

de Wet, C. F. (2006). Beyond presentations: Using PowerPoint as an effective instructional tool. *Gifted Child Today, 29*(4), 29–39.

Dickinson, D. (1995). Multiple technologies for multiple intelligences. In R. Fogarty & J. Bellanca (Eds.), *Multiple intelligences: A collection.* Arlington Heights, IL: IRI/Skylight Training and Publishing.

Done, P. (2006). Make 'em laugh (& they'll learn a lot more). *Instructor, 115*(7), 32, 34–35.

Dougherty, E. (2012). *Assignments matter: Making the connections that help students meet standards.* Alexandria, VA: ASCD.

Duckor, B., & Holmberg, C. (2017). *Mastering formative assessment moves: 7 high-leverage priorities to advance student learning.* Alexandria, VA: ASCD.

DuFour, R. (2015). *In praise of American educators: And how they can become even better.* Bloomington, IN: Solution Tree.

Erlauer, L. (2003). *The brain-compatible classroom: Using what we know about learning to improve teaching.* Alexandria, VA: ASCD.

Fisher, D., & Frey, N. (2019). The micro-teaching advantage: Videotaping a teacher's practice makes for a better debrief, and more learning. *Educational Leadership, 76*(5), 82–83.

Fogarty, R. (1990). *Designs for cooperative interactions.* Thousand Oaks, CA: Corwin.

Frey, N., Fisher, D., & Smith, D. (2019). *All learning is social and emotional: Helping students develop essential skills for the classroom and beyond.* Alexandria, VA: ASCD.

Frey, N., Hattie, J., & Fisher, D. (2018). *Developing assessment-capable visible learners, K–12: Maximizing, skill, will, and thrill.* Thousand Oaks, CA: Corwin.

Garmston, R. (2019). *The astonishing power of storytelling: Leading, teaching, and transforming in a new way.* Thousand Oaks, CA: Corwin.

Garmston, R., & Wellman, B. (1992). *How to make presentations that teach and transform.* Alexandria, VA: ASCD.

Garmston, R., & von Frank, V. (2012). *Unlocking group potential to improve schools.* Thousand Oaks, CA: Corwin.

Gewertz, C. (2007). Diplomas count: Ready for what? Preparing students for college, careers, and life after high school. *Education Week, 26*(40), 25–27.

Glazer, S. (2006, August). A good icebreaker. *Teaching Pre K–8, 37*(1), 86–87.

Green, J. (2002). *The green book of songs by subject—A thematic guide to popular music* (5th ed.). Nashville, TN: Professional Desk Reference.

Grinder, M. (2000). *A healthy classroom.* Battle Ground, WA: Michael Grinder & Associates.

Gunter, H., Estes, T., & Schwab, J. (1999). *Instruction: A models approach* (3rd ed.). Needham Heights, MA: Allyn & Bacon.

Hall, P., & Simeral, A. (2015). *Teach, reflect, learn: Building your capacity for success in the classroom.* Alexandria, VA: ASCD.

Hall, P., & Simeral, A. (2017). *Creating a culture of reflective practice: Capacity-building for schoolwide success.* Alexandria, VA: ASCD.

Hannaford, C. (2005). *Smart moves: Why not all learning is in your head* (2nd ed.). Salt Lake City, UT: Great River Books.

Harvey, S., & Goudvis, A. (2007). *Strategies that work: Teaching comprehension for understanding and engagement.* Portland, ME: Stenhouse.

Harwayne, S. (2001). *Writing through childhood: Rethinking process and product.* Portsmouth, NH: Heinemann.

Hattie, J. (2012). *Visible learning for teachers: Maximizing impact on learning.* New York, NY: Routledge.

Hattie, J., & Clarke, S. (2019). *Visible learning feedback.* New York, NY: Routledge.

Hoff, R. (1992). *"I can see you naked."* Kansas City, MO: Andrews and McMeel.

Hornfischer, J. D. (2016). *The fleet at flood tide: America at total war in the Pacific, 1944–45.* New York, NY: Bantam Books.

Jenkins, L. (2008). *From systems thinking to systemic action: 48 key questions to guide the journey.* Lanham, MD: Rowman & Littlefield.

Jensen, E. (2000a). *Learning with the body in mind.* Thousand Oaks, CA: Corwin.

Jensen, E. (2000b). *Music with the brain in mind.* San Diego, CA: The Brain Store.

Jensen, E. (2005a). *Teaching with the brain in mind* (2nd ed.). Alexandria, VA: ASCD.

Jensen, E. (2005b). *Top tunes for teaching: 977 song titles & practical tools for choosing the right music every time.* San Diego, CA: The Brain Store.

Jensen, E. (2007). *Introduction to brain-compatible learning* (2nd ed.). Thousand Oaks, CA: Corwin.

Johnson, D. W., Johnson, R. T., & Holubec, E. J. (1990). *Circles of learning: Cooperation in the classroom.* Edina, MN: Interaction Book Company.

Johnston, P. H., Bennett, T., & Cronin, J. (2002). I want students who are thinkers. In R. L. Allington & P. H. Johnston (Eds.), *Reading to learn: Lessons from exemplary fourth-grade classrooms* (pp. 140–165). New York, NY: Guilford Press.

Jones, F. (2007). *Tools for teaching* (2nd ed.). Santa Cruz, CA: Fredric H. Jones & Associates.

Juliani, A. J. (2018). *The PBL playbook: A step-by-step guide to actually doing project-based learning.* Write Nerdy Publishing.

Kagan, S. (1994). *Cooperative learning.* San Clemente, CA: Kagan Cooperative Learning.

Keene, E. O., & Zimmermann, S. (2007). *Mosaic of thought: The power of comprehension strategy instruction* (2nd ed.). Portsmouth, NH: Heinemann.

Lemke, C. (2010). Innovation through technology. In J. Bellanca & R. Brandt (Eds.), *21st century skills: Rethinking how students learn* (pp. 243–272). Bloomington, IN: Solution Tree.

Lent, R. C. (2012). *Overcoming textbook fatigue: 21st century tools to revitalize teaching and learning.* Alexandria, VA: ASCD.

Lipman, D. (1999). *Improving your storytelling: Beyond the basics for all who tell stories in work or play.* Atlanta, GA: August House Publishers.

Lipton, L., & Wellman, B. (2000). *Pathways to understanding: Patterns and practices in the learning-focused classroom* (3rd ed.). Guilford, VT: Pathways Publishing.

Maguire, J. (1998). *The power of personal storytelling: Spinning tales to connect with others.* New York, NY: Jeremy P. Tarcher/Putnam.

Marcarelli, K. (2010). *Teaching science with interactive notebooks.* Thousand Oaks, CA: Corwin.

Marzano, R. (2007). *The art and science of teaching: A comprehensive framework for effective instruction.* Alexandria, VA: ASCD.

Marzano, R. (2019). *The handbook for the new art and science of teaching.* Alexandria, VA: ASCD.

McTighe, J., & Seif, E. (2010). An implementation framework to support 21st century skills. In J. Bellanca & R. Brandt (Eds.), *21st century skills: Rethinking how students learn* (pp. 149–172). Bloomington, IN: Solution Tree.

Medina, J. (2008). *Brain rules: 12 principles for surviving and thriving at work, home, and school.* Seattle, WA: Pear Press.

Nash, R., & Hwang, K. (2013). *Collaborative school leadership: Practical strategies for principals.* Lanham, MD: Rowman & Littlefield.

Nathanson, S. (2006). Harnessing the power of story: Using narrative reading and writing across content areas. *Reading Horizons,* 47(1), 1–26.

National Commission on Writing for America's Families, Schools, and Colleges. (2006). *Writing and school reform, including the neglected "R": The need for a writing revolution.* Retrieved from http://www.collegeboard.com/prod_downloads/writingcom/writingschool-reform-natl-comm-writing.pdf

Nelson, B. (1996). Cooperative learning. *The Science Teacher,* 63(5), 22–25.

Ollerenshaw, J., & Lowery, R. (2006). Storytelling: Eight steps that help you engage your students. *Voices From the Middle,* 14(1), 30–31, 34–37.

Parry, T., & Gregory, G. (1998). *Designing brain-compatible learning.* Arlington Heights, IL: Skylight Professional Development.

Peters, T. (2018). *The excellence dividend: Meeting the tech tide with work that wows and jobs that last.* New York: Vintage.

Pfeffer, J., & Sutton, R. I. (2000). *The knowing-doing gap: How smart companies turn knowledge into action.* Boston, MA: Harvard Business School Press.

Posey, A. (2019). *Engage the brain: How to design for learning that taps into the power of emotion.* Alexandria, VA: ASCD.

Prensky, M. (2010). *Teaching digital natives: Partnering for real learning.* Thousand Oaks, CA: Corwin.

Reagan, R. (2009). Cognitive composition: Thinking-based writing. In A. Costa & B. Kallick (Eds.), *Habits of mind across the curriculum: Practical and creative strategies for teachers.* Alexandria, VA: ASCD.

Rief, L. (2003). *100 quickwrites: Fast and effective freewriting exercises that build students' confidence, develop their fluency, and bring out the writer in every student.* New York, NY: Scholastic.

Ritchhart, R., Church, M., & Morrison, K. (2011). *Making thinking visible: How to promote engagement, understanding, and independence for all learners.* San Francisco, CA: Jossey-Bass.

Rivers, S. E., Hagelskamp, C., & Brackett, M. A. (2013). In J. H. McMillan (Ed.), *SAGE handbook of research on classroom assessment* (pp. 347–366). Thousand Oaks, CA: SAGE.

Robinson, K. (2011). *Out of our minds: Learning to be creative.* Chichester, England: Capstone.

Rogers, S., & Renard, L. (1999). Relationship-driven teaching. *Educational Leadership,* 57 (1), 34–37.

Rowe, M. (1986). Wait time: Slowing down may be a way of speeding up! *Journal of Teacher Education,* 37(1), 43–50.

Ruiz-Primo, A. C., & Li, M. (2013). Examining formative feedback in the classroom context: New research perspectives. In J. H. McMillan (Ed.), *SAGE handbook of research on classroom assessment* (pp. 215–232). Thousand Oaks, CA: SAGE.

Schmidt, L. (2002). *Gardening in the minefield: A survival guide for school administrators:* Portsmouth, NH: Heinemann.

Smith, R. (2004). *Conscious classroom management: Unlocking the secrets of great teaching.* Fairfax, CA: Conscious Teaching Publications.

Sprenger, M. (2002). *Becoming a "wiz" at brain-based teaching.* Thousand Oaks, CA: Corwin.

Stiggins, R., & Chappuis, J. (2012). *An introduction to student-involved assessment for learning* (6th ed.). Boston, MA: Pearson.

Syed, M. (2015). *Black box thinking: Why most people never learn from their mistakes—but some do.* New York: Penguin.

Sylwester, R. (1995). *A celebration of neurons: An educator's guide to the human brain.* Alexandria, VA: ASCD.

Tate, M. (2003). *Worksheets won't grow dendrites.* Thousand Oaks, CA: Corwin.

Tate, M. (2007). *Shouting won't grow dendrites.* Thousand Oaks, CA: Corwin.

Tate, M. (2012). *"Sit & get" won't grow dendrites.* Thousand Oaks, CA: Corwin.

Trelease, J. (2006). *The read-aloud handbook* (5th ed.). New York, NY: Penguin.

Trilling, B., & Fadel, C. (2009). *21st century skills: Learning for life in our times.* San Francisco, CA: Jossey-Bass.

Twenge, J. M. (2017). *iGen: Why today's super-connected kids are growing up less rebellious, more tolerant, less happy, and completely unprepared for adulthood.* New York, NY: Atria Books.

Walsh, J., & Sattes, B. (2011). *Thinking through quality questioning: Deepening student engagement.* Thousand Oaks, CA: Corwin.

Wagner, T., & Dintersmith, T. (2015). *Most likely to succeed: Preparing our kids for the innovation era.* New York: Scribner.

Whitaker, T. (2004). *What great teachers do differently: 14 things that matter most.* Larchmont, NY: Eye on Education.

White, K. (2017). *Softening the edges: Assessment practices that honor K–12 teachers and learners.* Bloomington, IN: Solution Tree.

White, M. (2000). *Leonardo: The first scientist.* New York, NY: St. Martin's Press.

Wicks, C., Peregoy, J., & Wheeler, J. (2001). *Plugged in! A teacher's handbook for using total quality tools to help kids conquer the curriculum.* New Bern, NC: Class Action.

Wiggins, G. (2012). Seven keys to effective feedback. *Educational Leadership, 70*(1), 11–16.

Wiliam, D. (2018). *Embedded formative assessment.* Bloomington, IN: Solution Tree.

Wolfe, P. (2001). *Brain matters: Translating research into classroom practice.* Alexandria, VA: ASCD.

Wolk, S. (2008, October). School as inquiry. *Phi Delta Kappan, 90*(2), 115–122.

Wong, H., & Wong, R. (2005). *How to be an effective teacher: The first days of school.* Mountain View, CA: Harry K. Wong Publications.

Wubbels, T., Levy, J., & Brekelmans, M. (1997). Paying attention to relationships. *Educational Leadership, 54*(7), 82–86.

Zacarian, D. (2013). *Mastering academic language: A framework for supporting student achievement.* Thousand Oaks, CA: Corwin.

Zwiers, J. (2008). *Building academic language: Essential practices for content classrooms.* San Francisco, CA: Jossey-Bass.

Zwiers, J., & Crawford, M. (2011). *Academic conversations: Classroom talk that fosters critical thinking and content understandings.* Portland, ME: Stenhouse.

Index

editing and feedback, 81
interactive notebooks, 84, 85
learning logs, 81–82
literacy skills, 28
online learning platforms, 78–79, 81
peer relationships, 77, 78, 81, 86–87, 126
quickwrites, 78, 85
reading and speaking impacts, 78, 85–86
reflective blogs, 82–83
reflective journals, 77, 82

room arrangements, 79
think-write-pair-share instructional strategy, 92–93
topic choice, 79–81, 83–84
use of music, 77, 92–93
Wubbels, T., 20

Z
Zacarian, D., 28, 85
Zimmermann, S., 78
Zwiers, J., 11, 29, 34, 36, 126

CORWIN

A SAGE Publishing Company

CORWIN HAS ONE MISSION: to enhance education through intentional professional learning.

We build long-term relationships with our authors, educators, clients, and associations who partner with us to develop and continuously improve the best evidence-based practices that establish and support lifelong learning.